NEW MEXICO

NEW MEXICO BY ROAD

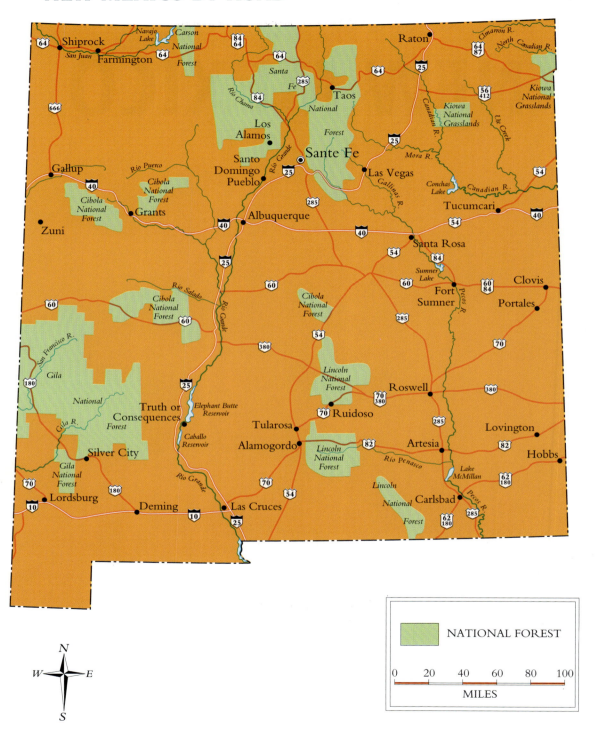

NATIONAL FOREST

0   20   40   60   80   100
MILES

N
W · E
S

CELEBRATE THE STATES

NEW MEXICO

Melissa McDaniel

***B*ENCHMARK *B*OOKS**

MARSHALL CAVENDISH
NEW YORK

For Mary and Willis McDaniel

Benchmark Books
Marshall Cavendish Corporation
99 White Plains Road
Tarrytown, New York 10591-9001

Copyright © 1999 by Marshall Cavendish Corporation

Library of Congress Cataloging-in-Publication Data
McDaniel, Melissa.
New Mexico / Melissa McDaniel.
p.   cm.   — (Celebrate the states)
Includes bibiographical references (p.   ) and index.
Summary: Discusses the geographic features, history, government, people,
and attractions of the state known as the "Land of Enchantment."
ISBN 0-7614-0659-X
1. New Mexico—Juvenile literarture. [1. New Mexico.] I. Title. II. Series.
F796.3.M34   1999   978.9—dc21   98-26425   CIP   AC

Maps and graphics supplied by Oxford Cartographers, Oxford, England

Photo research by Candlepants Incorporated

Cover photo: The Image Bank / Nicolas Russel

The photographs in this book are used by permission and through the courtesy of: *Ralph Lee Hopkins:* 6-7, 17, 18, 99, 114, back cover. *The Image Bank:* Eric Schweikardt, 14; Marc Romanelli, 20, 76; MacDuff Everton, 26-27; A. M. Rosario, 57; Larry Gatz, 62; Place, 66-67; Michael Melford, 71(right); John Lewis Stage, 72; T. Stableford, 96-97; Pete Turner, 110; Lisl Pennis, 122; Nick Nicholson, 129. *Randall K. Roberts:* 10-11, 13, 15, 22, 60; 63, 70(left), 70-71, 79, 80, 103, 104, 105, 108, 109, 113, 117, 119, 138. *National Agricultural Library:* 23. *Photo Researchers, Inc.:* David T. Roberts, 24(top); Tom McHugh, 24(bottom); Spencer Grant, 52-53; Alexander Tsiaras/Science Source, 59; R. Rowan, 75, 126; Porterfield Chickering, 82-83; Leonard Lee Rue, 123(right); Phil A. Dotson, 123(left); *Collection the Gerald Peters Gallery, Santa Fe, New Mexico:* 28-29. *Federal Postal Service/Paintings by Gerald Cassidy:* 32, 33. *The Bancroft Library, University of California accession #1961.020:5-A:* 38. *Courtesy Museum of New Mexico:* Painting by Gerald Cassidy, 39; #28539, 41(left); #113653, 43. #5889, 48; photo by Wyatt Davis #44191, 93. *Rose Collection, Western History Collections, University of Oklahoma Library:* 41(top), 45. *National Atomic Museum:* 50. *Archive Photos:* 47, 87, 91, 131, 132, 133, 136. *Jack Parsons:* 73. *Horst Tappe/Archive Photos:* 85. *Falk/New York Times/ Archive Photos:* 90. *Corbis Bettmann:* 89, 94. *W. P. Fleming/Adstock:* 107.

Printed in Italy

5   6   4

CONTENTS

NEW MEXICO IS . . .

New Mexico is stunning landscape . . .

"The scenery is so beautiful, I have to face the wall in order to concentrate on my writing."　　　　　—author Judy Blume

"[It] is a perfectly mad looking country—hills and cliffs and washes too crazy to imagine all thrown up in the air by God and let tumble where they would."　　　　　—artist Georgia O'Keeffe

. . . under extraordinary sky.

"There was so much sky, more than at sea, more than anywhere else in the world. . . . Even the mountains were made ant-hills under it. Elsewhere the sky is the roof of the world; but here the earth was the floor of the sky."　　　　　—novelist Willa Cather

New Mexico is captivating.

"Here . . . everything was intensified for one—sight, sound, and taste—and I felt that perhaps I was more awake and more aware than I had ever been before."　　　—arts patron Mabel Dodge Luhan

"The moment I saw the brilliant, proud morning shine high over the deserts of Santa Fe, something stood still in my soul, and I started to attend."　　　　　—writer D. H. Lawrence

A century ago, many visitors found New Mexico a strange and exotic land . . .

"Before I had gone six blocks up the narrow crooked streets lined with low adobes, I began to doubt that I was in the United States of America."   —Clyde Kluckhohn, visitor in the 1920s

. . . but some newcomers were less than charmed.

"It is the most miserable squalid looking place I ever beheld. The houses are mud, the fences are mud, the churches & courts are mud, in fact it is *all* mud."   —Anna Maria Morris, Santa Fe, 1850

Today, many New Mexicans maintain strong links to the past.

"My village is still undeveloped. We're about a hundred years behind schedule. We're not in a hurry. Life's too short, so why rush it."   —lifelong resident of Las Trampas

---

The old and the new come together in New Mexico. The world's leading scientific research laboratories lie just down the road from the ruins of ancient Indian cities. Outdoors enthusiasts who just moved to the state rub shoulders with rugged ranchers carrying on a way of life they inherited from their great-grandparents. Recent arrivals mingle with proud Hispanics whose ancestors came to New Mexico four hundred years ago and Native Americans whose families have lived in the same spot since before Europeans even knew North America existed. It is this combination of new and old and older yet that gives New Mexico its unique character and has earned it the name Land of Enchantment.

1 EARTH AND SKY

The first time people visit New Mexico, they often wonder what all the fuss is about. All they see is bleak, dusty earth. But then they spy a fascinating red rock formation in the distance. They notice the dark beauty of the rugged mountains and the magical glow over the everchanging vistas. They gradually realize that New Mexico's seemingly empty moonscape is all the more extraordinary because it teems with wildlife. By this time, there's no turning back—they too have fallen under New Mexico's spell.

MOUNTAINS, DESERTS, AND PLAINS

New Mexico has some of the most varied landscape in the United States. In its southwestern corner, jagged mountain ranges alternate with dry desert regions. You can drive across miles of flat, dry land, then suddenly see sharp mountain spires looming ahead. As you ascend the steep roads to the range's peaks, the temperature drops quickly, and the desert landscape gives way to lush ponderosa pine and Douglas fir trees.

While the mountain forests offer a cool retreat from New Mexico's parched land, the arid regions are just as beautiful and interesting. In some places, scrubby creosote bushes dot the land so evenly that they look like they were planted that way. The deserts are particularly striking in the spring, when plants burst into

Cactus blooms bring splashes of color to New Mexico's desolate countryside.

bloom. Bright yellow flowers sprout from the tops of the flat, round prickly pear cactus branches. The long ocotillo stems come alive with red blossoms. The bloom of the yucca, New Mexico's state flower, is spectacular. From the middle of its circle of pointed fronds, a stalk shoots five feet into the air, topped with a huge constellation of white flowers.

The eastern third of New Mexico is part of the Great Plains, the rolling grasslands that stretch from North Dakota to Texas. The section of the plains along New Mexico's eastern edge is some of the flattest land on Earth. This region, called the *Llano Estacado*, or Staked Plain, stretches into the Texas Panhandle. In this barren land, there are no hills and no trees, nothing but scrubby grass. The Llano Estacado may have been named by early European travelers who pounded stakes into the ground to show which way they had come—otherwise they would have lost their way because the landscape looked exactly the same in every direction.

Although many people find the Llano Estacado dull and oppres-

Much of New Mexico is vast open flatlands.

Strange spires rise in the Bisti Badlands.

sive, some who live and work there revel in its emptiness. The only dwelling on a ranch owned by one elderly couple is a shack with no running water. Yet they stay on the land. "I like the peace and quiet," the woman says.

Northwestern New Mexico contains some of the state's most dramatic landscapes. Craggy mesas and abrupt bluffs are scattered across the dusty plains. In many places, soft sandstone has worn

LAND AND WATER

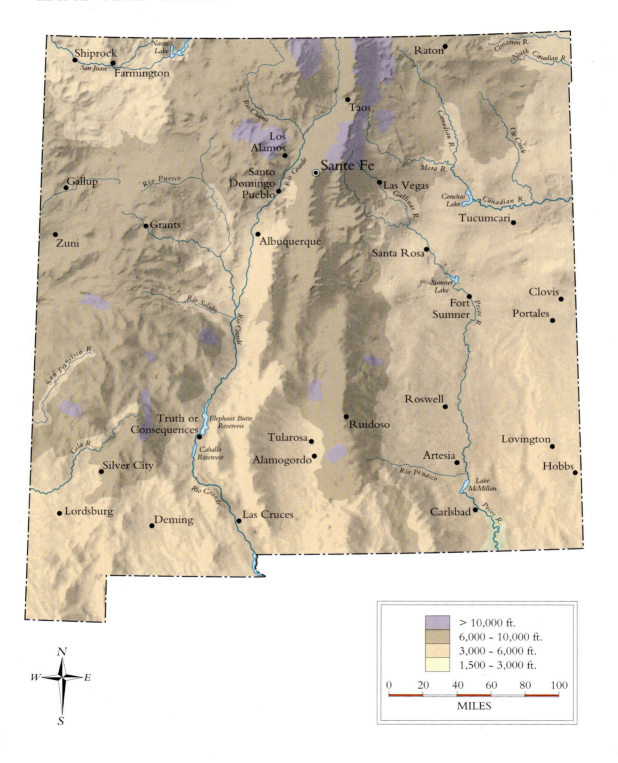

Shiprock
Navajo Lake
San Juan
Farmington
Rio Chama
Raton
Cimarron R.
North Canadian R.
Canadian R.
Taos
Los Alamos
Rio Grande
Sante Fe
Canadian R.
Ute Creek
Gallup
Rio Puerco
Santo Domingo Pueblo
Mora R.
Las Vegas
Gallinas R.
Conchas Lake
Canadian R.
Grants
Albuquerque
Tucumcari
Zuni
Santa Rosa
Rio Salado
Sumner Lake
Fort Sumner
Pecos R.
Clovis
Portales
San Francisco R.
Rio Grande
Roswell
Gila R.
Truth or Consequences
Elephant Butte Reservoir
Ruidoso
Lovington
Tularosa
Artesia
Hobbs
Caballo Reservoir
Alamogordo
Silver City
Rio Penasco
Lake McMillan
Lordsburg
Rio Grande
Carlsbad
Pecos R.
Deming
Las Cruces

	> 10,000 ft.
	6,000 – 10,000 ft.
	3,000 – 6,000 ft.
	1,500 – 3,000 ft.

0   20   40   60   80   100
MILES

N
W   E
S

away over thousands of years into odd forms. One of the most amazing areas is the Bisti Badlands, a region of twisting pillars and mushroom-shaped formations set among colorful cliffs. Walking among the bizarre spires, it seems as if you've landed on another planet.

In north-central New Mexico lie the Jemez and the Sangre de Cristo Mountains, the two southernmost ranges of the Rocky Mountains. Their steep slopes are dotted with rocky outcrops and

The Jemez Mountains are one of the lushest parts of New Mexico, filled with rushing streams and pine forests.

Late in the day, the Sangre de Cristo Mountains give off a warm glow.

ponderosa pine, spruce, and aspen trees. The Sangre de Cristo, which means "blood of Christ" in Spanish, were named for the reddish color they turn as the day's light wanes. Writer Bill Bryson says these mountains "are just sensational . . . especially at sunset when they simply glow, as if lit from within, like jack-o'-lanterns."

Flowing between the two ranges is the Rio Grande, New Mexico's backbone. It runs all the way down the middle of the state from Colorado to just south of Las Cruces, before curving east to become the border between Texas and Mexico. Indians built their villages along the Rio Grande, as did European settlers. As the largest river in a state where riverbeds often run dry, the Rio Grande brings life.

THE ENDLESS SKY

New Mexico's landscape is much more than mountains, rivers, and deserts. What lures visitors back time and again is the sky. On the state's vast flatlands, where nothing blocks the view, the sky seems larger than it does elsewhere. Even in the mountains, where the horizon is not as distant, the sky captivates. "Everyone always talks about the sky around Taos, and it is astonishing," Bryson once remarked. "I had never seen a sky so vivid and blue, so liquid."

The quality of the light and intensity of the colors make New Mexico's sky unique. Sometimes it almost seems like you can reach out and grab the air. "It's the most beautiful sky in the world," said one woman who moved to New Mexico. "It makes you dream. It's like a movie, always changing. It has wonderful colors, and you can lose yourself in the openness."

At night the sky is equally bewitching. Many parts of New

"The sky is all-embracing and all-pervading," critic Elizabeth McCausland
once said of New Mexico. *"The sky is always present."*

Mexico are far from any city lights, so after nightfall countless stars
are visible in the clear, dark skies. Sometimes the nights are so
black and the stars so bright that you don't even need a flashlight
to walk about. You can make your way by the glare of the Milky Way
galaxy, even if the moon is not up.

SUN AND SNOW

New Mexico's climate is as varied as its landforms. More than
twenty-five feet of snow falls each year in some mountainous areas,

while the state's desert regions receive only a few inches of rain. Where rain does fall, it often comes in buckets in the summer during violent afternoon thunderstorms. These storms sometimes dump so much water that the parched earth cannot absorb it all. Instead, the water courses over the land in dangerous flash floods.

Much of New Mexico is known for its pleasant climate. Days are warm and dry, nights cool and comfortable. Southern New Mexico's mild winters have prompted many people to retire there. Even in January, towns such as Roswell reach an average high of 56 degrees. During the summer, the southeastern corner of the state can be scorching. After the sun sets, however, the temperature quickly drops.

In the north, winter lasts more than half the year. One disgruntled early traveler wrote that New Mexico's climate is "eight months of winter and four months of hell." But while winters are long and cold, they are also bright and sunny. In Santa Fe the sun shines more than three hundred days a year. Blinding snowstorms are often followed by dazzling blue skies, creating a lovely, sparkling landscape. One New Jerseyite who moved to Santa Fe says, "This is the only winter I ever remember when I wasn't longing for spring."

When spring finally comes it brings spectacular wildflower displays and strong winds. The wind picks up speed moving across New Mexico's unbroken expanses, keeping the Southwest's famous tumbleweeds bobbing along until they pile up against fences and buildings. Because the state is so dry and dusty, the wind causes unusual problems. Instead of warning of possible ice on the road, some New Mexico highways have signs warning of dust storms.

Northern New Mexico's long winters provide plenty of opportunity to ski.

WILD THINGS

New Mexico is full of wildlife. Even in cities such as Santa Fe, bears, mountain lions, and skunks occasionally wander into town. Naturally, you have a better chance of seeing animals if you get off the pavement and into the wilds. Elk, deer, porcupines, and bighorn sheep live in the forests. The state's deserts and dry prairies are home to jackrabbits, coyotes, and javelinas, large creatures

SMOKEY BEAR

Of all the creatures that have ever roamed through New Mexico, none is more famous than Smokey Bear. In 1950, a smoldering cigarette started a devastating forest fire in the south-central part of the state. After firefighters put out the blaze, they discovered a tiny black bear cub hanging on for dear life high up in a scorched pine tree. The creature was badly burnt. They named him Smokey.

Although the Forest Service had invented the character Smokey Bear to help prevent forest fires a few years earlier, it wasn't until a real Smokey showed up that the campaign sprang to life. Soon, everyone in the country knew about Smokey and the motto "Only *you* can prevent forest fires." The program was spectacularly successful. Before Smokey, 30 million acres of forest and rangeland burned in the United States each year. By the 1970s, that number had dropped to 1 million. Smokey had become so popular and received so much mail that he was given his own zip code.

After Smokey had been discovered and his burns were treated, one of his rescuers took him home. The man soon concluded that even baby bears don't make good pets, so Smokey went off to live at the National Zoo in Washington, D.C. After he died in 1976, he was buried in the village of Capitan, near where he had been found.

Rattlesnakes live throughout New Mexico. At some parks, signs warn, "Respect rattlesnakes' privacy—please stay on trail."

Roadrunners eat insects, lizards, gophers, and even rattlesnakes.

that look like wild boars and love munching on prickly pear cacti. Rattlesnakes live among the rocks throughout New Mexico. Their bite can be dangerous, but like most animals, they won't bother you if you don't bother them.

New Mexico also abounds with birds. Hawks soar high overhead, eyeing prey. Finches, thrashers, warblers, and woodpeckers flit among the trees. In the southern half of the state, huge black vultures circle slowly over the roads and fields, searching for an easy meal. New Mexico's most famous bird, the roadrunner, grows up to two feet long, half of it tail, and has a fluffy crest of feathers atop its head. Although roadrunners can fly, they spend most of their time on the ground. It is not unusual to see them racing down the road, sometimes reaching speeds of twenty miles an hour.

The Bosque del Apache National Wildlife Refuge, in the southwest, is a paradise for birds and bird-watchers. More than three hundred species of birds can be seen in these wetlands, including herons, egrets, and ducks. Winter is an especially good time to visit, because tens of thousands of snow geese, thousands of sandhill cranes, and even a few bald eagles and delicate, endangered whooping cranes come down from colder climes in the north.

PRESERVING THE LAND

In recent years, New Mexico has become a battleground between ranchers who want to use the land and environmentalists who want to protect it. Much land in New Mexico is owned by the government. Ranchers often lease this public land to graze their cattle. Sometimes, cattle are allowed to overgraze, destroying the

willow and cottonwood forests along streams and leaving behind barren, crumbling riverbanks. Some birds that nest in these areas have become endangered. Today, there are fewer than one thousand Southwestern willow flycatchers left. According to Jennifer Fowler-Propst of the U.S. Fish and Wildlife Service, "Their habitat is being lost at an astonishing rate."

Some environmentalists want to halt all grazing on public lands. So much damage has been done, they argue, that it is the only way to stop these once-green areas from becoming desert. Many ranchers feel picked on. Time and again environmental organizations are "telling people in New Mexico how to run their business," complains Erik Ness of the New Mexico Farm & Livestock Bureau.

In New Mexico, ranchers and environmentalists are frequently at odds over cattle grazing.

They argue that they are just trying to make a living, as their parents and grandparents did before them. "This business is ingrained, it's a part of you, and somebody comes and takes that away from you. They might as well take your life," says rancher Kit Laney, who has fought hard to continue grazing on public land.

People on both sides are calling for compromise, although sometimes it's hard to hear them above the din of angry voices. Most ranchers know it is in their economic self-interest to take care of the land. Rick Johnson of the Nature Conservancy says the only way to have healthy stream systems "is for everyone to work together." Only time will tell whether ranchers and environmentalists will find a way to protect the land that they both love.

2 A COLORFUL PAST

Northern New Mexico, by Carlos Vierra

Although New Mexico was one of the last states admitted to the Union, it has a long and colorful history. Many people don't realize that before the English established their colonies on the East Coast, Spaniards had already built villages in the New Mexican wilderness. And before that—a thousand years ago—Indians had constructed fabulous cities there.

THE ANCIENT ONES

Humans have been living in what is now New Mexico for about 12,000 years. In the eastern grasslands, ancient peoples pursued the camels, giant bison, and huge, elephant-like creatures called mammoths that once lived there. As the New Mexican climate became drier, these large mammals died out or headed north where food was more plentiful.

New Mexico's early inhabitants turned to hunting smaller animals and gathering fruits, nuts, and berries to survive. Over time, they began growing corn, squash, and beans. Having a regular supply of food allowed them to build permanent villages. The Mogollon were the first group to settle in one place.

New Mexico's best-known early Native Americans are called the Anasazi, a Navajo Indian word that means "the ancient ones" or "enemy ancestors." Between about A.D. 900 and 1300, the Anasazi constructed great villages out of rocks, which they fit together so precisely that the mud mortar they used was often unnecessary. Some Anasazi buildings were five stories high and had hundreds of rooms. The Anasazi sometimes built irrigation systems to water the fields of corn that surrounded their cities. They also made elegant pottery decorated with intricate patterns. Over time, the Anasazi developed the most complex civilization north of present-day Mexico.

But then something happened. The Anasazi abandoned their cities. No one is sure why, but most likely, a severe drought that lasted from 1276 to 1299 forced them off the land. Many headed toward the Rio Grande Valley, where water was more plentiful. They mixed with Pueblo Indians who already lived there. *Pueblo* is a Spanish word meaning "village." The Pueblo came to be called that because, like the Anasazi, they lived in towns. The Pueblo Indians lived in houses of rock or adobe, a mixture of earth and straw that has been baked in the sun. In nearby fields, they grew corn, squash, and melons.

In about 1500, the Navajo and the Apache Indians migrated to the Southwest from present-day Canada. The Navajos settled west of the Pueblos, who taught them how to grow corn and beans. The Apaches, who spread out over what is now eastern and southern New Mexico, were great hunters and warriors.

THE SPANIARDS ARRIVE

Soon, other people wandered into the Southwest. The Spaniards who had conquered the Indians in Mexico in 1521 spent much of

The Zuñi were the first Native Americans to encounter Spanish explorers in present-day New Mexico.

their time searching for precious metals. Legend had it that far to the north, beyond great swaths of desolate, unknown land, were the Seven Cities of Cíbola, towns so wealthy that the streets were paved with gold.

In 1539, a party led by Father Marcos de Niza set out in search of the fabled cities. After trudging nearly two thousand miles, they neared Zuñi Pueblo, in present-day western New Mexico. When the Indians killed one member of the party, the rest hurried back to Mexico. Father Marcos told the Spanish authorities what they wanted to hear: that the Zuñi lived in magnificent villages larger than Mexico City.

The following year, Francisco Vásquez de Coronado led an expedition to Zuñi to uncover the riches of Cíbola. When they arrived there they found nothing but mud huts. Father Marcos "has not told the truth in a single thing that he has said," Coronado wrote bitterly.

The Indians told Coronado that the riches were farther east, most likely just to get rid of him. An Indian guide who led Coronado through the empty plains kept telling him that fabulous

Coronado traveled thousands of miles in search of Cíbola, the fabled city of gold, only to be disappointed.

COYOTE BRINGS WINTER: A ZUNI TALE

This is one of the many Native American tales featuring the untrustworthy Coyote.

One day, back when the earth was still new, Eagle and Coyote were out hunting together. They came to the pueblo of the Kachinas, who had a box in which they kept the sun. Whenever the Kachinas wanted light, they opened the box a crack and the sun peeked out. Then it was day.

"This is wonderful," Coyote said. "Let's steal the box."

"No, that would be wrong," said Eagle. "Let's just borrow it."

When no one was looking, Eagle grabbed the box and flew off. Coyote followed along the ground. He said to Eagle, "Let me carry the box. I am ashamed to let you do all the carrying."

"No, I don't trust you," Eagle answered. "You might open the box and lose this wonderful thing we have borrowed."

Coyote asked again and again, until Eagle finally relented. "You must promise not to open the box," Eagle said.

"I promise," Coyote declared.

When they entered a wooded area, Coyote ducked behind a bush where Eagle could not see him and opened the box. The sun burst out and flew away to the edge of the sky. At once the world grew cold. Leaves fell from the trees and icy winds blew.

"I should have known better," Eagle said to Coyote. "I should have remembered you never keep a promise. If you had not opened the box, we could have kept the sun near us. We would have had summer all the time. Now we have winter."

cities lay just over the horizon. The expedition traveled as far as present-day Kansas, where they came upon a Wichita Indian village. Again, there was nothing but huts. Furious at being led on a wild goose chase, Coronado ordered the guide killed. He returned to Mexico City disappointed and disgraced.

Forty years passed before the Spaniards bothered to return to the Rio Grande Valley. Brief forays were made into the region in the 1580s and early 1590s. Then, in 1598, Juan de Oñate led a group north to settle New Mexico. They established a village near where the Chama River flows into the Rio Grande and began searching for riches and trying to convert the Indians to Christianity.

Not all Pueblo Indians took kindly to being converted. The Acomas lived in a village atop a 357-foot-high mesa. The only way up was by steep uneven stairs worn into the rock; everywhere else was sheer cliff. The Acomas felt secure in their fortress in the sky. In 1598, a skirmish between the Acomas and Oñate's nephew Juan de Zaldivar left Zaldivar and about a dozen other Spaniards dead. Oñate was outraged. He ordered his men to "burn [Acoma] to the ground, and leave no stone on stone, so that the Indians may never be able again to inhabit it." Oñate's men killed eight hundred Indians. The Acomas who survived the massacre hardly fared better. Adults were sentenced to twenty years' slavery, and every man over twenty-five not only was enslaved but also had one foot cut off. The Acoma would never forget this horrifying slaughter.

Around 1610, Oñate was called back to Mexico City, where he was tried and convicted of mistreating the Indians. That same year the Spanish colonists moved to another spot farther south. They called it Santa Fe. Founded just three years after the settlement of

Jamestown, Virginia, the first permanent English settlement in the New World, Santa Fe is the oldest capital city in the United States.

THE PUEBLO REVOLT

In the following decades, the Spaniards solidified their control over the Rio Grande Valley. They grew crops, raised livestock, and tried to turn the Pueblo Indians into Spaniards. They made the Indians take Spanish names and speak only Spanish. They forced them to work in Spanish fields, repair roads, and dig ditches. Worst of all, the Spaniards banned the Indians' religion. They prohibited Indian dances, burned religious objects, and destroyed kivas, the buildings where Pueblos held sacred ceremonies. Indians who continued to practice their religion were whipped, jailed, and sometimes murdered.

Finally, the Indians rebelled. A medicine man named Popé, who had been imprisoned and whipped, coordinated a revolt among all the Pueblos. On August 10, 1680, Indians stormed through the countryside, burning churches and killing priests. "The god of the Spaniards is dead," they shouted, "but our gods will never die." Then they moved toward Santa Fe. For nine long days, a battle raged. After four hundred Spaniards had been killed, the remaining colonists fled south toward Mexico. For the first and last time, Native Americans had driven out their European conquerors.

The Indians then tried to erase every shred of evidence that the Spaniards—and their religion—had ever been there. They destroyed Spanish clothing, tools, and animals. They bathed in rivers, trying to scrub off their Christian baptisms. But they could not turn back the clock. After Popé died, the Spaniards easily retook the colony in 1692. The Pueblo Indians would never again be totally independent.

Although the Spaniards were back in control, they had learned from their defeat. They still expected Indians to become at least outwardly Christian, but they no longer destroyed kivas and Indian religious objects. They realized that a more peaceful approach would make life easier for everyone.

THE GROWING COLONY

During the next century, the young colony grew slowly, as more settlers traveled north from Mexico. By 1800, ten thousand New Mexicans lived along the northern Rio Grande.

Although technically New Mexico was ruled by officials in Mexico City, those officials were more than a thousand miles away. The New Mexicans basically governed themselves. Surrounded on all sides by vast empty lands, New Mexicans knew little of events taking place elsewhere, such as the birth of the United States far away on the East Coast. According to historian Ruth Armstrong, "The American Revolution might have just as well been on another planet for all the difference it made to the Spaniards of New Mexico."

New Mexico's isolation enabled it to develop a unique society. Over the years many Spaniards and Indians married and had children. In New Mexico, people of mixed ancestry were accepted and could hold important jobs. Many became prominent members of the community, which would have been impossible in Mexico or Spain.

Although a few New Mexicans owned vast ranches, most lived

A New Mexican horseman rides by adobe houses.

on small farms where they raised just enough crops and livestock to feed themselves. Since Spain didn't allow its colonies to trade with foreign countries, including the United States, any goods that the settlers couldn't make themselves had to be brought up from Mexico, which took many weeks.

Then, in 1821, Mexico declared itself independent from Spain. New Mexico was now part of a new country. The Mexican government immediately decided to allow trade with the United States. That same year, a merchant named William Becknell crossed the

Great Plains from Missouri with clothing, knives, and other goods. In Santa Fe, the New Mexicans eagerly bought all his wares. Becknell made another trip the following year, and the Santa Fe Trail was born. In the coming years, many fortunes were made by traders who traveled the harsh eight-hundred-mile trail to sell furniture, glassware, candles, and books to the New Mexicans.

BECOMING AMERICAN

The United States and Mexico went to war over a boundary dispute in 1846. That August, American general Stephen Kearny led an

After Mexico became independent from Spain, American merchants began making the long trek from Missouri to Santa Fe to sell their goods.

army into New Mexico. Facing no resistance from the locals, he climbed to a rooftop in the town of Las Vegas and announced that New Mexico was now part of the United States. This was made official two years later in the Treaty of Guadalupe Hidalgo. From then on, Anglos would join Hispanics and Indians in building New Mexico's unique society.

In 1862, General James Carleton was sent to New Mexico to subdue the Navajos and Apaches, who had been raiding settlers' farms. Carleton minced no words about what he was doing. "There is to be no council held with the Indians, nor any talks," he ordered. "The men are to be slain whenever and wherever they can be found. The women and children may be taken prisoners, but, of course, they are not to be killed."

Carleton commanded Colonel Kit Carson to round up the Indians and move them onto the Bosque Redondo Reservation on New Mexico's eastern plains. Carson was a complicated man. His wife was from a prominent Hispanic family, and he got along well with New Mexico's Indians. He didn't like Carleton's policies, but he obeyed orders. When the Navajos refused to move, Carson's men burned their homes, slaughtered their sheep, and destroyed their fields. Facing starvation, the Navajos had little choice but to surrender.

In 1864, thousands of Navajos began trudging three hundred miles to Bosque Redondo in what became known as the Long Walk. With little food and inadequate clothing, their journey over snowy mountains and frozen plains turned into a disaster. Hundreds died. The trek was so horrible that to this day, the Navajos date historical events by whether they happened before or after the Long Walk.

Kit Carson was in charge of the brutal campaign to force the Navajos and Apaches onto the Bosque Redondo Reservation.

Many Indians starved to death at Bosque Redondo because not enough food could be grown on the arid land.

Conditions on the reservation were no better. Many died of starvation and disease. Eventually, U.S. officials had no choice but to admit that their policies had failed and allow the Navajos and Apaches to return to reservations in their homelands.

THE WILD WEST

Gradually, Americans trickled into what must have seemed a strange and dangerous land. Some planted crops in the fertile valleys. Others sought their fortunes mining silver and gold in the mountains. John Chisum made a fortune, but not from precious metals. Cattle made Chisum rich. In the 1870s, he grazed 80,000 cattle on eastern New Mexico's broad plains, which likely made him the biggest cattle rancher in the country.

New Mexico's growing towns were overrun by cowboys, miners, railroad workers, gamblers, and cattle rustlers—but they did not always have sheriffs to keep the peace. Still an isolated frontier, New Mexico was as wild as anywhere in the West. Most men wore guns and were more than willing to use them. Emerson Hough, a writer at the time, said New Mexico "was without doubt, as dangerous a country as ever lay out of doors." The northeastern town of Cimarron was particularly notorious. One newspaper reported, "Everything is quiet in Cimarron. Nobody has been killed in three days."

Throughout New Mexico, power struggles erupted in violence. In 1878, a feud between rival merchants turned Lincoln County red with blood. The most famous participant in this bloodbath was Billy the Kid. Billy was born in Brooklyn, New York, moved west

Most men wore guns in frontier New Mexico.

at age thirteen, and was arrested and escaped from jail for the first time at fifteen. His gangly charm and explosive temper were legendary. According to Sheriff Pat Garrett, who eventually killed him, the Kid's "face always wore a smile. He ate and laughed, drank and laughed, rode and laughed, talked and laughed, fought and laughed—and killed and laughed."

The Kid was convicted of murdering the Lincoln County sheriff, but before he could be hanged, he escaped, killing two deputies

BILLY THE KID

William H. Bonney, who came to be known as Billy the Kid, was born in New York City on November 23, 1859. His family moved west, and he eventually found himself in Silver City, New Mexico. Over the years his reputation as a cold-blooded killer grew and grew until he was shot to death by his former friend Sheriff Pat Garrett on July 14, 1881. Then legend took over and portrayed him as a folk hero.

go, Where a man's on-ly friend was his old for-ty four.

When Billy the Kid was a very young lad,
In old Silver City he went to the bad.
Way out in the West with a gun in his hand,
At the age of twelve years he killed his first man.

Young Mexican maidens play guitars and sing
Songs about Billy, their boy bandit king,
How there's a young man who had reached his sad end—
Had a notch on his pistol for twenty-one men.

It was on the same night when poor Billy died,
He said to his friends, "I'm not satisfied.
There are twenty-one men I have put bullets through—
Sheriff Pat Garrett must make twenty-two."

Now this is how Billy the Kid met his fate,
The bright moon was shining the hour was late.
Shot down by Pat Garrett who once was his friend,
The young outlaw's life had now reached its sad end.

Now there's many a lad with a face fine and fair,
Who starts out in life with a chance to be square,
But just like poor Billy they wander astray,
They lose their life in the very same way.

on the way out. When Garrett gunned him down two months later, Billy the Kid was twenty-one years old.

THE LONG ROAD TO STATEHOOD

New Mexico's reputation for lawless chaos often prompted people to repeat General William Tecumseh Sherman's joke that "The United States ought to declare war on Mexico and make it take back New Mexico." From the time New Mexico became U.S. territory, politicians in Washington had railed against granting political equality to New Mexicans, the majority of whom were Hispanic. "Ours, sir, is the Government of a white race," roared Senator John C. Calhoun of South Carolina. As the years passed, many people remained suspicious of New Mexico, where people spoke a different language and enjoyed different customs. They argued that New Mexicans could never be true Americans. Again and again, New Mexico was denied statehood.

Only with the Spanish-American War in 1898, when the United States helped the island nation of Cuba throw off Spanish rule, did these attitudes finally change. Some people had questioned whether New Mexicans, many of whom were of Spanish descent, would be loyal to the United States. The New Mexicans answered them loud and clear. Half of Theodore Roosevelt's famous Rough Riders Regiment were New Mexicans. By the war's end, they had proven themselves so loyal, so brave, that no one could doubt their commitment to America. Finally, in 1912, after sixty-two long years as a territory, New Mexico became the forty-seventh state.

As the century progressed, more and more people found reason

"VIVA VILLA!"

In the early hours of the morning of March 9, 1916, a band of Mexican revolutionaries led by the famed general and bandit Pancho Villa crept over the border into the town of Columbus, New Mexico. For years, Mexico had been in chaos, with various factions vying for power. President Woodrow Wilson had recognized one of Villa's enemies, Venustiano Carranza, as the official leader of Mexico. Villa was angry.

The rebels wreaked havoc on Columbus. Amid shouts of "Viva Villa, viva Mexico!" ("Long live Villa, long live Mexico"), they burned houses, shot citizens, and collected whatever guns, ammunition, and other supplies they could find. After members of the U.S. Cavalry stationed nearby awoke, the battle was on. By the time dawn broke, the Mexicans had retreated south, and Columbus was in smoldering ruins. Eighteen Americans and about ninety Mexicans had been killed. It was the first and only time in the twentieth century that a foreign force invaded the United States.

President Wilson sent General John Pershing and over six thousand soldiers into Mexico to capture Villa, but they were no match for the harsh Mexican terrain. After chasing Villa for almost a year, Pershing returned home empty-handed, ending the strange saga of the sacking of Columbus.

New Mexican Rough Riders taking an oath of allegiance in Santa Fe

to venture to New Mexico. Some came because their doctors told them the clear air would cure tuberculosis, a deadly lung disease. Painters, photographers, and writers were drawn by the state's blinding beauty. The military discovered that New Mexico's uncluttered plains were ideal for air force bases.

TO THE PRESENT

In 1943, a group of newcomers took over the Los Alamos Ranch School in the Jemez Mountains. Hundreds of people who got off the train in Santa Fe and were whisked to the remote site did not even know where they were being taken. Each was given a driver's license with a number instead of a name. Their project was so secret that only people who couldn't read were hired to empty their garbage cans.

They had been brought together to develop the atomic bomb, the most destructive weapon the world has ever known. The United States was in the midst of World War II and believed it had to make the bomb before its enemies did.

On July 16, 1945, the secret of what all those people were doing in the mountains was revealed. In the desert of south-central New Mexico, the world's first atomic bomb was detonated. The blinding orange flash was visible in Santa Fe, nearly 150 miles away. At the blast site, temperatures as hot as that of the sun caused the sand to melt into glass. In a nearby bunker, Robert J. Oppenheimer, the project's leader, muttered an ancient Hindu quotation, "I am become Death, destroyer of worlds." Within a month, atomic bombs had leveled the Japanese cities of Hiroshima and Nagasaki. World War II was over, but everything had changed. The nuclear age had arrived.

New Mexico profited greatly from the nuclear age, as military bases and research laboratories multiplied within its borders. The state's growing economy and warm, dry climate attracted throngs of newcomers. By the 1950s, Albuquerque, the state's largest city, was bursting at the seams. "New houses go up in batches of fifty to three hundred at a time, and transform the barren mesas before you get back from lunch," one journalist commented.

In the decades since, newcomers have continued to flock to the

One man who observed the world's first atomic bomb being detonated in central New Mexico said it was like "the grand finale of a mighty symphony . . . fascinating and terrifying, uplifting and crushing."

state. But no matter how much New Mexico grows, its rich past is always evident. New roads pass right by pictures etched into rocks by Indians a thousand years ago. As New Mexico moves into the twenty-first century, old-timers and newcomers alike honor its long and colorful past.

3 GROWING AND CHANGING

The capitol in Santa Fe

New Mexico's government is based on its state constitution, which was adopted in 1911. Most sections of the constitution can be changed if a majority of voters agree. But out of respect for the state's unique history, changing sections that protect the voting rights and education of Spanish-speaking people requires a larger majority. Two-thirds of the voters in each county and three-quarters of the voters as a whole must agree.

INSIDE GOVERNMENT

Like the federal government and those of other states, New Mexico's government has three divisions: executive, legislative, and judicial.

Executive. The head of New Mexico's executive branch is the governor, who is elected to a four-year term. Before a bill passed by the legislature becomes law, the governor must sign it. He or she also appoints many important state officials, such as some members of the board of finance.

Legislative. New Mexico's legislature is made up of forty-two senators, who are elected to four-year terms, and seventy representatives, who are elected to two-year terms. The legislature proposes and votes on bills. If a majority of both the senate and the house of representatives votes for a bill and the governor signs it,

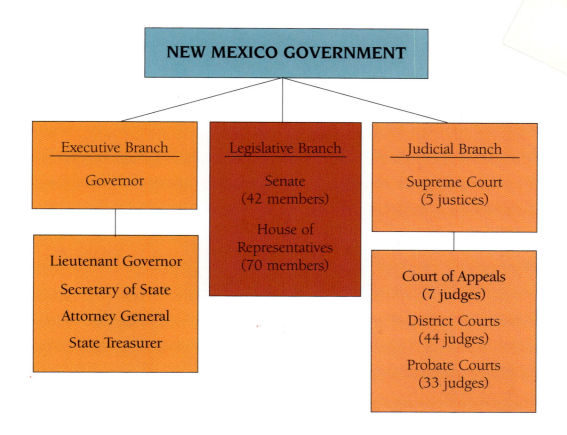

NEW MEXICO GOVERNMENT

Executive Branch

Governor

Lieutenant Governor

Secretary of State

Attorney General

State Treasurer

Legislative Branch

Senate
(42 members)

House of
Representatives
(70 members)

Judicial Branch

Supreme Court
(5 justices)

Court of Appeals
(7 judges)

District Courts
(44 judges)

Probate Courts
(33 judges)

it becomes law. If the governor vetoes, or rejects, the bill, it can still become law if enough legislators vote to override the veto.

Judicial. New Mexico's highest court is the supreme court, which has five justices who are elected to eight-year terms. The supreme court determines whether laws enacted by the legislature violate the state constitution. The justices also decide whether cases from lower courts were handled properly. The state's primary trial courts are called district courts. If someone disagrees with a decision in a district court, he or she can ask the court of appeals to review it. Most cases heard by the court of appeals can also be appealed to the supreme court.

GREEN POLITICS

Traditionally, most New Mexicans have been Democrats. But as more outsiders have flocked to the state to work in high-tech industries or enjoy the sunshine, Republicans have grown in power.

In recent years, the rise of the Green Party has complicated the situation. The Green Party's primary concern is protecting the environment. In 1997, Republican Bill Redmond was elected to the U.S. House of Representatives from the heavily Democratic district that covers northern New Mexico. Carol Miller, the Green Party candidate, earned 17 percent of the vote—votes that normally would have gone to the Democrats—allowing Redmond to win with just 43 percent. While Republicans were crowing over their victory, Democrats were fuming. "A lot of people are mad at the Greens," says Sam Baca of Santa Fe. "They don't have a chance of winning, and they just serve to elect Republicans."

The Greens respond that neither major political party has done enough for the environment, and that working for what you believe in is the American way. Miller says, "We are stimulating democracy, helping the United States reach a more diverse political situation." Although the Greens have enough followers to win races in Santa Fe and Taos Pueblo, it remains to be seen whether they can attract the vote necessary to win in larger areas.

GROWING CITIES

As New Mexico's sunshine and clean air draw more and more people to its cities, the problems these cities face grow and change. In the last few years, muggings, robbery, and vandalism have become increasingly common in Santa Fe. Some people think this is inevitable. "Crime is a problem partly because the population is growing," says city councilor Cris Moore.

While Santa Feans are troubled by graffiti and purse snatchings, Albuquerque residents worry about drive-by shootings and stolen cars. To combat the rising crime rate, police are trying to teach people how not to be crime victims. They say that using common sense usually keeps people out of trouble. Still, many folks in smaller

Although Santa Fe has grown in recent years, it still has many peaceful, adobe-lined streets.

communities around the state remain wary of Albuquerque. "You can't even go out after dark there," says a Tucumcari woman whose daughter lives in Albuquerque.

Albuquerque also faces other problems. As its population has grown, the city has spread into the surrounding hills and plains, replacing piñon trees and cacti with housing developments and strip malls. This sprawl strains the government, which must build roads and provide services to ever more distant communities. And since more and more commuters drive farther and farther to work each day, the developments contribute to air pollution. "We now understand as a community that if we continue to sprawl, we won't be able to either service the new areas or improve our air quality," says one local official.

To try to slow the sprawl, the city is encouraging developers to build in empty sites within the city rather than in previously undeveloped areas. Albuquerque is also trying to persuade stores and businesses to locate near homes, so people can walk to where they want to go, rather than always having to get in the car. With government and business working together, hopefully Albuquerque will continue to grow and prosper without polluting the air that draws people to it.

MAKING A LIVING

The U.S. government is a major employer in New Mexico. For decades, the military has been taking advantage of the state's flat, dry expanses to build air force bases and testing fields. Los Alamos National Laboratories and Sandia National Laboratories,

New Mexico is a center for advanced scientific research. Here, a man works with a particle-beam fusion accelerator.

which is Albuquerque's largest employer, are among the world's leaders in scientific research.

Tourism is also vital to the New Mexican economy. More than twelve million people visit the state each year to enjoy its ski slopes, cafés, pueblos, and caves. They provide motel owners, shopkeepers, craftspeople, and cooks with a living. But sometimes the people who live off tourism resent these outsiders coming in and taking over their towns, clogging their streets and driving up prices. "A lot of people don't like the tourism, but at the same time, there's nothing else," says Andrea Lopez, who runs a fajita stand

Santa Fe's Latino heritage is celebrated throughout the year.

in Santa Fe. Still, she sees tourism as preferable to industry, which might harm the environment. Although little manufacturing takes place in Santa Fe, elsewhere in the state New Mexicans make computer chips, telephone equipment, scientific instruments, appliances, and printed materials.

Many ranchers graze cattle and sheep on the sparse vegetation that grows on New Mexico's plains, but the dry, rocky soil makes farming difficult. In the eastern part of the state, irrigation has enabled farmers to grow hay, wheat, and cotton. Along the Rio Grande, pecans and chiles are leading crops. The town of Hatch is a center for chile production. In late summer and early fall, the main road through Hatch is lined with shacks selling the freshest and tastiest chiles around.

Farming is a hard way to make a living. Between late freezes that destroy crops and falling prices that eliminate profits, uncertainty is the norm. "Sometimes, I get so disgusted and depressed that I feel like quitting," says Orlando Casados Jr., a chile farmer near the town of Española. "But come spring, you just feel like getting out there on the tractor and doing it all over again. Chile is our heritage. I just think that somewhere along the line, if we keep up the tradition, it will pay off." His father, Orlando Sr., who started the farm, agrees that working the land is worth the headaches. "Farming is a nice little life," he says. "You never get rich, but it's a nice little life."

GROSS STATE PRODUCT: $5.2 BILLION

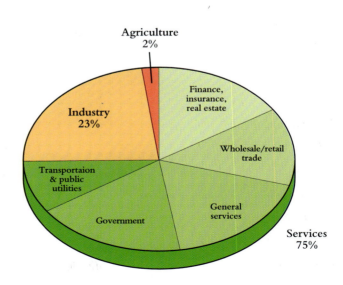

Agriculture
2%

Finance,
insurance,
real estate

Industry
23%

Wholesale/retail
trade

Transportaion
& public
utilities

General
services

Government

Services
75%

(2000 estimated)

RECIPE: SALSA

Chile peppers give New Mexico's spicy food its fire. Some kinds of chiles are much hotter than others. A scale called Scoville units tells how much burn a chile has. Bell peppers have no fire and barely register on the scale. Jalapeños score 5,000. But that's nothing compared to habaneros, which soar to between 200,000 and 300,000 Scoville units.

Chiles are an important ingredient in salsa, a delicious concoction New Mexicans can't get enough of. They put it on everything—eggs, tacos, hamburgers. Of course it's good with chips, too.

Choose your chile based on how hot you like your food (habaneros are definitely not a good idea). Have an adult help you with this recipe:

2 medium tomatoes
1 medium onion
1 clove garlic
½ teaspoon salt
2 green chiles

Peel the chiles and remove their seeds. Chop the chiles, tomatoes, and onions finely. (Wash your hands after handling chiles.) Crush the garlic and blend it with the salt. Mix everything together. Let sit for about an hour so the flavors can mingle. Enjoy—on anything!

Blood-red strings of chile peppers, called ristras, are a common sight at roadside stands in New Mexico.

The first Spaniards who came to New Mexico were searching for gold and silver. Although they didn't find any, vast riches were hidden beneath the earth. New Mexico is among the leading states in the production of natural gas, oil, and potash, which is used in making fertilizer. New Mexico also has more copper in the ground than almost any other state. Three hundred million pounds of

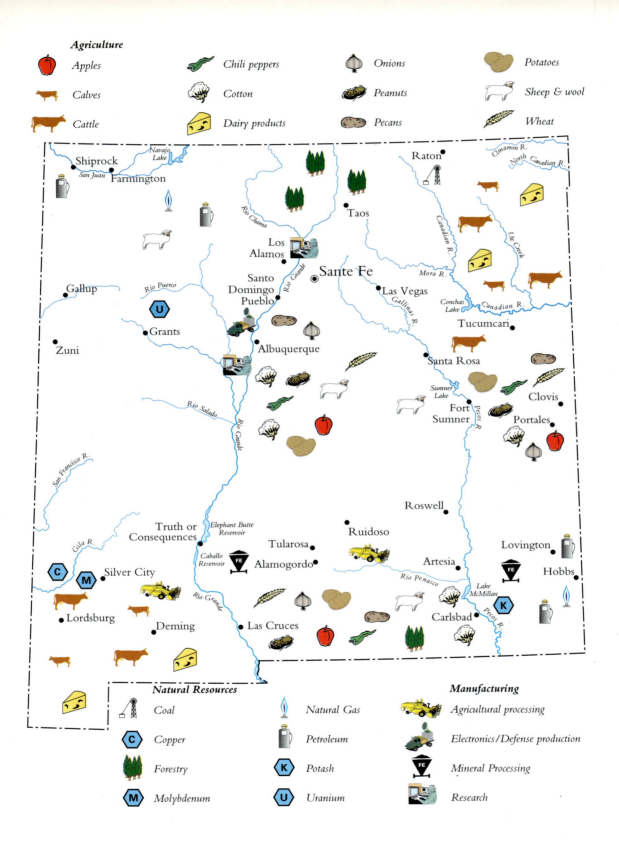

Agriculture

Apples
Calves
Cattle
Chili peppers
Cotton
Dairy products
Onions
Peanuts
Pecans
Potatoes
Sheep & wool
Wheat

Shiprock
Farmington
San Juan
Navajo Lake
Rio Chama
Taos
Raton
Cimarron R.
North Canadian R.
Canadian R.
Ute Creek
Los Alamos
Santo Domingo Pueblo
Rio Grande
Sante Fe
Las Vegas
Gallinas R.
Mora R.
Conchas Lake
Canadian R.
Tucumcari
Gallup
Rio Puerco
Zuni
U
Grants
Albuquerque
Rio Salado
Rio Grande
Santa Rosa
Sumner Lake
Fort Sumner
Pecos R.
Clovis
Portales
San Francisco R.
Roswell
Truth or Consequences
Elephant Butte Reservoir
Caballo Reservoir
Gila R.
Silver City
C
M
Lordsburg
Deming
Rio Grande
Tularosa
Alamogordo
FE
Las Cruces
Ruidoso
Artesia
Rio Penasco
Lake McMillan
Carlsbad
Pecos R.
Lovington
FE
Hobbs
K

Natural Resources

Coal
Copper — C
Forestry
Molybdenum — M
Natural Gas
Petroleum
Potash — K
Uranium — U

Manufacturing

Agricultural processing
Electronics/Defense production
Mineral Processing — FE
Research

copper are removed each year from the Santa Rita copper mine, one of the oldest operating mines in North America. Today, it is a mile-wide canyon, and the town of Santa Rita that used to sit atop it is long gone.

CHANGING WITH THE TIMES

As New Mexico's economy changes, its cities are forced to change with it. For instance, mining towns are quickly deserted when there is no more ore in the ground. After World War II, Madrid, once a thriving coal mining town, became a ghost town, a jumble of tattered buildings with broken windows. In the early 1970s, the coal company that owned all the buildings in town auctioned them off. In just a few days, artists and others who wanted to escape to a place where they could live very cheaply bought every building. Today, 80 percent of Madrid's three hundred residents are artists, "a higher percentage than any other town in the country," one boasted. Madrid is a thriving community, its streets lined with shops, galleries, and cafés, a testament to a town's ability to reinvent itself.

Opposite:
EARNING A LIVING

4 PROUD TRADITIONS

Several different groups, each with its own proud history and traditions, have contributed to New Mexico's distinct character. Today, Anglos are the majority, but just barely. More than 38 percent of New Mexicans are of Hispanic descent, the highest percentage of any state in the Union. New Mexico also has the largest percentage of Native Americans among the states—about 9 percent. The state has a growing number of blacks and Asians as well. Over the centuries, these groups have mingled to form a culture unique to New Mexico.

THREE CULTURES

New Mexico's Native Americans have had more success maintaining their languages, religions, and traditions than Indians in other parts of the United States. Today, young Indians may work in the laboratories of Los Alamos and then return to their villages to participate in ceremonies during feast days.

Some New Mexican Indians continue to practice the arts passed down from their parents and grandparents. The Navajo are renowned for their beautiful woven rugs and turquoise jewelry. Apache baskets are prized.

The Pueblos are famous for their pottery. Each village has its own style of pottery. Some use many colors; others are black and white.

ETHNIC NEW MEXICO

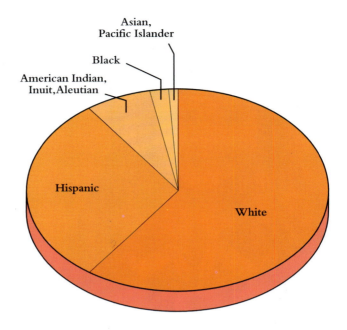

Asian, Pacific Islander

Black

American Indian, Inuit, Aleutian

Hispanic

White

While some decorate their pots with geometric designs, others look to nature for inspiration. For many Indians, pottery is more than a way to make a living. It is a vital part of their culture, a connection to the past. When Acoma Indians are born, they are bathed in a pottery bowl. When they die, they are buried with pottery. "We come into this world with pottery and we are going to leave the earth with pottery," says Acoma potter Dolores Garcia.

Pueblo Indians are known for their quiet hospitality. During festivals, they often invite total strangers, including tourists, into their homes for a meal. But visitors have not always been respectful enough of the Pueblos' ancient culture. "One thing I really get tired of is tourists looking at our villages like they were these miniature Disneylands where they can come in and gawk and do whatever they want," says a man from San Ildefonso Pueblo. "Don't get me wrong. We

New Mexico has a higher percentage of Native Americans than any other state.

Many Pueblo Indians are accomplished potters.

Dances are a highlight of Pueblo feast days.

PUEBLO FEAST DAYS

Pueblo Indians sometimes allow outsiders to visit during feast days. This is a great way to learn about their culture.

Often the celebrations mix traditional Pueblo religion with Christianity. On Christmas Eve at San Felipe Pueblo, the spirits of the animal kingdom come to honor the baby Jesus. In this striking ritual, deer dancers, wearing antler headdresses, step softly, while buffalo dancers, wearing horned headdresses and fur, stamp thunderously.

San Geronimo Day at Taos Pueblo features dancing and a trade fair, which includes displays of drums, pottery, and beaded moccasins. Young men participate in footraces. Black-and-white striped clowns wearing cornhusks in their hair climb a greased pole to reach bundles of food at the top and tease the people in the crowd. All in all, it is one of the most light-hearted Pueblo feast days.

New Mexican girls perform at a fiesta in Mesilla.

welcome people," he says. "But, please, . . . respect our way of life."

New Mexico's Hispanics are proud of their long history in the region. Many bristle when people from other parts of the country assume that their families must be recent immigrants because they are Spanish-speaking. They point out that their families were granted land in New Mexico by the Spanish crown long before the United States even existed. Today, some New Mexicans worry that the younger generations are forgetting their heritage. "Children

POPULATION GROWTH: 1860–2000

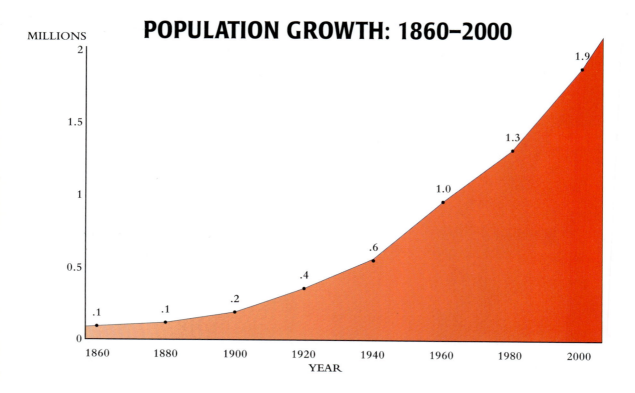

MILLIONS

YEAR

today do not speak Spanish—in my grandmother's house, we were not allowed to speak English," says Frank Ortiz, whose family has been in northern New Mexico since 1607. Although New Mexico's Hispanics have adapted to many changes over the centuries, their pride in their heritage is unwavering.

New Mexico's Anglos also have a colorful heritage to draw upon. It took courage and self-reliance for miners and cowboys to venture into this harsh, remote land. Their sons and daughters often exhibit a similar independent streak. "They can't make me wear a seatbelt, can't make me use matches that you strike on the box, and can't make me use a computer. I'm an old woman," says one seventy-year-old. Today, New Mexicans recall their frontier history in such events as Fort Sumner's Old Fort Days, which features a rodeo and a staged bank robbery.

SEARCHING FOR PARADISE

In recent decades, newcomers have swarmed into towns across New Mexico. Some are retired folks attracted by the state's pleasant climate and invigorating air. Others are wealthy Californians searching for a weekend getaway. Artists and others are looking for a beautiful

Young New Mexicans take a break from the heat at the Bell Ranch.

New Mexico's stark landscape has a powerful pull for many people. Writer Oliver LaFarge once called it "a land that draws and holds men and women with ties that cannot be explained or submitted to reason."

place where the cost of living is low. New Mexico's ridges, valleys, and rocky deserts make ideal refuges for people who have had it with city life, who want to be closer to nature and live in a simpler way. They also appeal to anyone who just wants to be left alone.

The influx of newcomers has changed many New Mexico towns. "Between when this town was founded in 1877 and 1995 the only place around here you could get wet was in the creek down there. Now there's three houses with swimming pools," says one Hillsboro resident. No matter why they come, the recent arrivals drive up land prices, often putting them out of the reach of longtime residents of New Mexico, which is among the poorest states in the nation.

Nowhere is this more true than in Santa Fe. Its dusty streets and adobe architecture have long charmed visitors, inspiring them to stay. Adobe houses are made of sun-dried bricks of earth and straw. Rough beams called vigas, which hold up the flat roof, stick all the way through the walls to the outside. Many people love adobe's warm feel and the way its brown curved shapes blend so easily into the landscape.

Although adobe is found all over New Mexico, it is most associated with Santa Fe. Practically every building in Santa Fe is some shade of brown. But these days, only the rich can afford real adobe. Many other houses that look like adobe are actually ordinary houses covered with stucco and painted brown. Often they have the corner fireplaces typical of real adobe houses. Some even have imitation vigas. Some people complain that Santa Fe has become a southwestern theme park. They call the town Santa Fake.

In 1990, for the first time Hispanics numbered less than half the city's population. "The white people moved in, painted the town brown and moved the brown people out," says former mayor Debbie Jaramillo. Priced out of their hometown, some Santa Feans have moved to Albuquerque, a more affordable city with better job opportunities. But many others love their town too much to abandon it and are trying to find ways to ensure that it serves all its residents, not just tourists and wealthy newcomers.

CELEBRATING TOGETHER

Every September the people of Santa Fe hold the Fiesta de Santa Fe to commemorate the Spaniards' return to the city after the Pueblo Revolt. The first fiesta was celebrated in 1712—no other community celebration in the United States goes back that far. During the fiesta, Santa Fe overflows with street dances, concerts, and processions. Parades featuring floats, low-rider cars, and children and their pets dressed in costume bring life and color to the city streets.

Christmas is a magical time in New Mexico. All over the state, people line streets and walls and rooftops with small paper bags containing glowing candles propped in sand. These decorations, called farolitos in northern New Mexico and luminarias in Albuquerque and farther south, create a lovely wavering orange light. In Santa Fe, tens of thousands of people step out into the chilly night air on Christmas Eve. They stroll around town, enjoying the flickering displays, sipping hot cider, and perhaps marveling at how lucky they are to live in a place that is truly enchanting.

VILLAGE LIFE

New Mexico is sprinkled with small towns and villages where the residents have deep roots and loyalties. In Las Trampas, a village

"BURN HIM!"

"Burn him, burn him," chant 40,000 Santa Feans one Friday evening. The object of their ill will is a forty-foot-tall wood and papier-mâché monster named Zozobra, also known as Old Man Gloom. Since 1926, Santa Feans have washed away their troubles and misfortunes by burning Zozobra.

As a fire dancer with a blazing torch circles the huge white puppet, the monster moans and groans, thrashes his arms and bobs his head, trying to scare the dancer off. But the fire dancer always wins, and the crowd gives a great cheer as Zozobra begins to burn. The monster's eyes turn glowing red and flames pour from his mouth. In three minutes, he is gone. Nothing remains but a wire framework and ashes wafting over the crowd.

With that, all the gloom of the previous year has been wiped away, and the Fiesta de Santa Fe is off and running.

between Santa Fe and Taos that is so small it doesn't even get a dot on many maps, most people are content to remain where their families have lived for hundreds of years. Just eighty people live in the town, but the population is not dropping, and very few outside families have moved in. Although some people go away to college or off to work elsewhere for a while, most eventually return,

At Christmas, farolitos, which are also called luminarias, line rooftops throughout New Mexico.

drawn home by the crisp air and the beautiful mountain scenery. "Everybody comes back," said Leroy Aguilar, whose family has lived in Las Trampas since the 1760s.

Although these tiny towns provide peace and a sense of community, living in them can be a challenge. Hillsboro, for instance, has no school, so children have to ride the bus more than thirty miles to the nearest town with a school. Hillsboro doesn't have many job opportunities either. When asked what people do there, one woman replied, "Well, there's ranching and there's a bar." Nor do these villages have the conveniences that most people expect. According to a shopkeeper in Las Trampas, "When you get old and sick, you have to move to Santa Fe because there's no medical services here. So then you have to leave, when you need to go to the doctor regularly."

Still, the man concludes, "Other than that, it's perfect. You gave me a million dollars, I wouldn't move away from here. It's my village. I belong here."

5 NOTABLE NEW MEXICANS

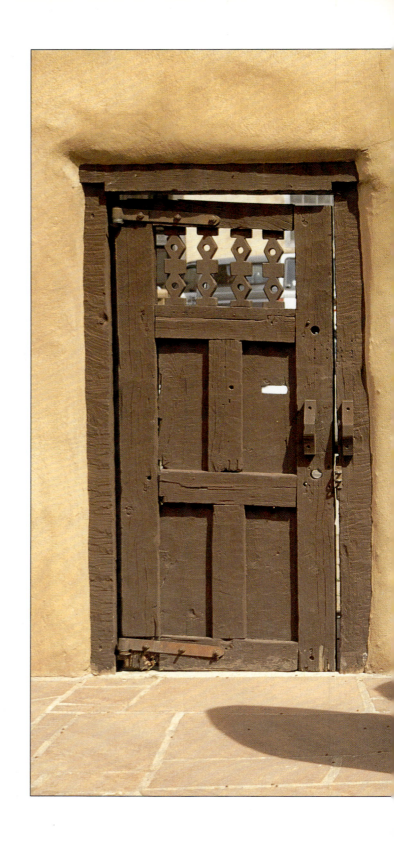

Ｎew Mexico has attracted many artists, writers, and scientists. Its subtle beauty inspires them, and its desert expanses give them room to create. New Mexico has also nurtured its own achievers, who have made their mark in every field.

WRITERS

Tony Hillerman has built a successful career by exploring Navajo society at the same time as he tells page-turning whodunits. Hillerman was born in the dirt-poor town of Sacred Heart, Oklahoma, in 1925. He was badly wounded fighting in Europe during World War II. While recovering in New Mexico, he saw a group of men on horses wearing face paint and feathers. They were Navajos performing a ritual to rid traces of war from returning soldiers. "To see people with a living culture still affecting how they live—that interested me," Hillerman explained. "I'm drawn to people who believe in something enough that their lives are affected by it."

Hillerman became a journalist and worked his way up to become executive editor at the *Santa Fe New Mexican* newspaper. He also spent many years teaching journalism at the University of New Mexico. When he finally began writing novels, his thoughts returned to the Navajos. In books such as *Skinwalkers* and *A Thief of Time*, Hillerman has examined Navajo traditions and problems

In 1987, the Navajos gave Tony Hillerman a Special Friend Award, "as an expression of appreciation and friendship for authentically portraying the strength and dignity of traditional Navajo culture."

with respect and understanding. As one of the country's most successful mystery writers, he has earned many awards. But he is most proud of the Special Friend Award he received from the Navajos, the only one they have ever given.

Another New Mexican writer, Rudolfo Anaya, uses his novels to examine his Hispanic heritage. Anaya, who grew up in a house where only Spanish was spoken, mined his own childhood for inspiration in writing *Bless Me, Ultima*, which is considered the classic novel about a Hispanic child growing up. "I tried to capture the old values and heritage of a village culture which was threatened with extinction," he has said.

THE FREEDOM OF THE LLANO

Rudolfo Anaya's novel *Bless Me, Ultima* tells the story of Antonio Marez, whose father is a vaquero—a cowboy—on New Mexico's empty plains.

My father had been a vaquero all his life, a calling as ancient as the coming of the Spaniard to Nuevo Méjico. Even after the big rancheros and the tejanos came and fenced the beautiful llano, he and those like him continued to work there, I guess because only in that wide expanse of land and sky could they feel the freedom their spirits needed. . . .

My mother was not a woman of the llano, she was the daughter of a farmer. She could not see the beauty in the llano and she could not understand the coarse men who lived half their lifetimes on horseback. After I was born in Las Pasturas she persuaded my father to leave the llano and bring her family to the town of Guadalupe where she said there would be opportunity and school for us. The move lowered my father in the esteem of his compadres, the other vaqueros of the llano who clung tenaciously to their way of life and freedom. There was no room to keep animals in town so my father had to sell his small herd, but he would not sell his horse so he gave it to a good friend, Benito Campos. But Campos could not keep the animal penned up because somehow the horse was very close to the spirit of the man, and so the horse was allowed to roam free and no vaquero on that llano would throw a lazo on that horse. It was as if someone had died, and they turned their gaze from the spirit that walked the earth.

DRIVE TO WIN

One New Mexican family has dominated the sport of auto racing for decades. Between them, Bobby and Al Unser have won the Indianapolis 500 seven times. The Unsers have racing in their blood. Their father and two uncles were racers, although none ever qualified for Indy. Since their father owned a garage in Albuquerque, the Unser boys grew up around cars. In 1958, their older brother Jerry became the first Unser to race in the Indianapolis 500. But at Indy the following year, he was in a horrible crash. He died from his injuries two weeks later.

Despite this tragedy, the brothers continued to pursue their favorite sport. If anything, Jerry's death made them more deter-

Bobby Unser won the Indianapolis 500 three times.

mined to succeed. Bobby raced in his first Indy 500 in 1963, and won his first in 1968. He retired in 1983, two years after his third Indy triumph, but Al kept on racing.

In 1983, Al and his son, Al Jr., became the first father and son to race in the same Indy 500. Two years later, they battled it out for the national championship. After losing the year-long competition to his father by a single point, Al Jr. remarked, "My dad taught me all I know about racing, but he hasn't taught me all he knows." Albuquerque has honored its hometown heroes by naming a major road Unser Boulevard.

Another competitor who has taken advantage of New Mexico's open spaces is Nancy Lopez, one of the greatest golfers ever and the first Mexican American on the Ladies Professional Golf Association (LPGA) circuit. Nancy Lopez moved from California to Roswell, New Mexico, shortly after her birth. By age seven, she was following her parents around golf courses, and before long she was racking up junior titles.

Although Nancy was the only girl on her high school golf team, she led the team to the state championship. In 1977, when she was just twenty years old, she turned professional and immediately broke the rookie earnings record for both men and women. The following year she won a record five tournaments in a row. With her radiant smile and friendly manner—not to mention her incredible talent—she soon had throngs of fans following her around the courses, cheering her as they had never cheered any golfer before. Tour attendance tripled. Over the years, Lopez has continued to collect wins. She has been named Player of the Year four times and has been inducted into the LPGA Hall of Fame.

Although Nancy Lopez has won dozens of tournaments, she is just as proud of the respect and affection that other players and fans have for her. "It is important to me to be a pleasant person," she has said.

EMPIRE BUILDER

Conrad Hilton, the founder of the Hilton Hotel chain, got his start in the tiny central New Mexico town of San Antonio, where he was born in 1887. When Conrad was a child, his father began renting out rooms of the family's adobe house for one dollar a day. As a

In the 1940s, Conrad Hilton bought many historic hotels. "I buy tradition and make the most of it," he once said.

teenager, Conrad was responsible for bringing traveling salesmen who had arrived late into town to the "Hilton inn." From these modest beginnings, young Hilton's career took off.

By 1919, Hilton was buying and building large hotels throughout Texas. In 1939, his attention returned to his home state. Although Albuquerque was still a backwater, he was convinced it was going to flourish, and he built a luxurious, ten-story hotel in the city's downtown. During the 1940s, Hilton purchased some of the most prominent hotels in the country, such as the Plaza and the Waldorf-Astoria in New York City. By his death in 1979, he had built a vast empire and was the most famous hotel man in the world.

ROCKET MAN

Rocket pioneer Robert Goddard was looking for a place to do his experiments—a flat, empty one. He had to have a lot of room to work so the noise and debris from his tests wouldn't bother anyone, as they sometimes had back home in Massachusetts. He also needed many clear, dry days, both so he could launch rockets year-round and because he was frequently sick and the healthy air would do him good. In the arid land outside Roswell, Goddard found the perfect spot.

By the time Goddard moved to New Mexico in 1930, he had already established himself as the world's foremost rocket scientist.

The research Robert Goddard carried out in his New Mexico workshop paved the way for travel to the moon.

Reading science fiction as a child, he had dreamed of ways to send rockets to the moon, and even to Mars, at a time when nobody took the possibility of space flight seriously. As early as 1919, Goddard suggested the possibility of a cone-shaped rocket fueled by a series of explosions. In 1926, he launched the world's first rocket that used liquid rather than solid fuel. It went just forty-one feet into the air, but it is considered as important to the development of rocketry as the Wright brothers' first airplane flight.

On New Mexico's barren plains, Goddard tinkered with his rockets. He figured out how to stabilize them and guide them, how to make them lighter, how to get them to go higher and faster. In the process, he developed an early jet engine. Goddard died in 1945, twenty-four years before rockets first carried men to the moon, but the technology that he had developed decades earlier helped send them there.

ARTISTS

Although New Mexicans have made their mark in many fields, the state is best known for its artists. Some of the state's greatest home-grown artists have been Pueblo potters, and among these none outshines Maria Martinez.

Martinez was born in San Ildefonso Pueblo, just north of Santa Fe, in the early 1880s. She learned about pottery from her aunt. "She didn't teach," Maria explained. "Nobody teaches pottery. . . . I used to go to visit my aunt and watch." Maria's husband, Julian, made the designs on her pots. They were already among the leading Pueblo potters when in the 1910s, they developed a special

Although Maria Martinez's black-on-black pots brought her worldwide fame, she was always modest, saying she "never cared about being well-known or anything."

method of firing that turned Maria's pots a shiny jet-black and Julian's designs a dull black. This black-on-black pottery would bring them fame. Many other San Ildefonso potters began making black-on-black pottery, but no one could match Maria's mastery. Her pots were thin, delicate, perfectly symmetrical, and rubbed to an extraordinary, glistening shine. Today, her pots are in museums all around the world. Although Martinez died in 1980, her legacy lives on, as her grandchildren, great-grandchildren, and great-great-grandchildren continue the family tradition.

New Mexico's intense light and luminous mountains have attracted countless painters, but none is more identified with the state than Georgia O'Keeffe. A pioneer of modern art, O'Keeffe was not satisfied to simply paint what she saw in a realistic way. She wanted to express something more. "If one could only reproduce nature," she once wrote, "and always with less beauty than the original, why paint at all?" O'Keeffe became famous for taking real-

Georgia O'Keeffe loved New Mexico. "I never feel at home in the East like I do out here," she once remarked.

istic subjects and abstracting them. In the process, she flooded the subjects with emotion. She painted flowers in extreme close-up, something no one had ever done before, which made the long lines of the petals boldly sensuous.

In 1929, O'Keeffe traveled to Taos, New Mexico, and was instantly enraptured. "No one told me it was like this!" she exclaimed. She had discovered the landscape that most inspired her. O'Keeffe spent much of the next half-century in New Mexico, painting the austere deserts, the glowing hills, the rivers cutting gorges through mountains. Again and again she painted the cliffs behind her house and the amazing adobe church in Ranchos de Taos.

But New Mexico gave her much more than the subject matter for her art. It gave her freedom. Living in a remote house, she rarely saw people. She spent her days tramping through the desert, driving her car through the hills, watching the light change. New Mexico's barren isolation allowed her to live her life the way she wanted to, as a fiercely independent woman.

6 OUT AND ABOUT IN NEW MEXICO

From north to south, and east to west, New Mexico is chock-full of the gorgeous, the fascinating, and the just plain weird.

THE SOUTH

Deep under southeastern New Mexico lies the state's most famous natural wonder, the Carlsbad Caverns, which is among the world's largest cave systems. The caverns were created over millions of years, as slightly acidic water dripped through cracks in a limestone mountain. Gradually, the water wore away the rock, creating large caverns. The seeping water also left behind little bits of minerals. Drop by drop, these minerals accumulated into extraordinary formations.

Walking into the Big Room is like stepping into a gigantic Dr. Seuss book—it seems too absurd for nature. Huge, gloopy formations are everywhere. Thin rods called soda straws hang from the ceiling and sometimes have small, round globs called popcorn attached to them. Ripply formations known as draperies are attached to some walls. Even today, constant dripping reminds visitors that some of the formations are still changing and growing.

People visit Carlsbad Caverns to see not only the wondrous underground world but also its famous bat colony. Between April and October, hundreds of thousands of Mexican free-tail bats make

Carlsbad Caverns is filled with remarkable formations.

their home there. Each evening, they spiral out of the cave entrance in a huge swarming tornado and head off for a night of feasting on insects. They return again at dawn, to spend the day sleeping in their favorite cavern.

Most people travel to New Mexico to gaze at wondrous mountains or explore ancient ruins; but some go to learn about aliens. The most famous alleged UFO sighting in American history occurred near Roswell, and the city has not one, but two museums dedicated to UFOs. At the International UFO Museum

THE ROSWELL INCIDENT

In 1947, a sheepherder stumbled across some debris on a ranch outside of Roswell. The U.S. Air Force gathered up the wreckage, examined it, and then issued an extraordinary press release saying they had found a flying saucer. The news shot around the world. The next day, the air force changed their tune—it was a weather balloon, they said. Fifty years later, many people still don't believe them.

Not everyone in Roswell is happy about the city's claim to fame. "Some people come up to me and say, 'Gosh, I don't like this. I don't want to be known as the kook capital,'" says local businessman Bill Pope. He reminds them that aliens equal money. Says Pope, "There's a little community not far from us over here that has lizard races. What it all comes down to is having something to create an interest in your community. . . . And that creates an inflow of people, and that creates dollars."

and Research Center, you might hear a "certified UFO investigator" claim that there are twenty different known species of aliens, some living among us. You can watch videos of people talking about their supposed alien encounters, and see photos of fuzzy objects that look like Frisbees. You can also buy lots of souvenirs.

Those Roswellians who haven't met any aliens often point to the Roswell Museum and Art Center as the best their city has to offer. The museum features an extensive collection of art by New Mexico's painters, potters, and sculptors, along with displays of Spanish armor and Indian artifacts. The museum's highlight is the exhibit devoted to rocket scientist Robert Goddard, who spent much of his

PLACES TO SEE

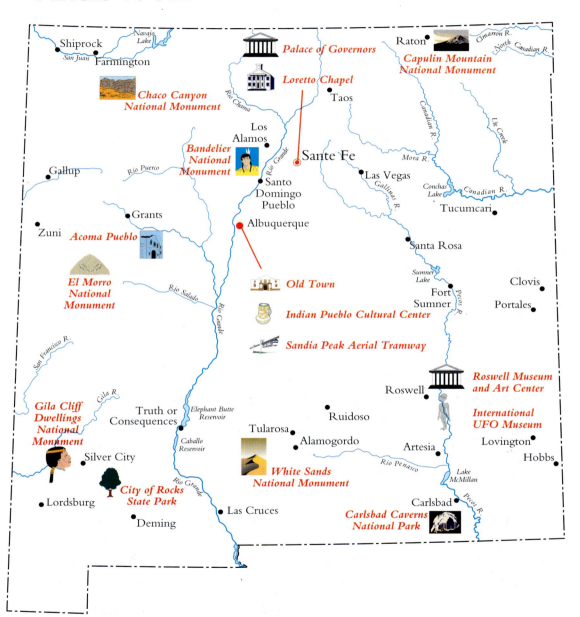

Shiprock

Navajo Lake

San Juan

Farmington

Chaco Canyon National Monument

Rio Chama

Palace of Governors

Loretto Chapel

Raton

Capulin Mountain National Monument

Cimarron R.

North Canadian R.

Taos

Canadian R.

Ute Creek

Los Alamos

Bandelier National Monument

Gallup

Rio Puerco

Rio Grande

Sante Fe

Santo Domingo Pueblo

Las Vegas

Mora R.

Conchas Lake

Canadian R.

Gallinas R.

Tucumcari

Zuni

Grants

Acoma Pueblo

Albuquerque

El Morro National Monument

Rio Salado

Rio Grande

Old Town

Indian Pueblo Cultural Center

Sandia Peak Aerial Tramway

Santa Rosa

Sumner Lake

Pecos R.

Fort Sumner

Clovis

Portales

San Francisco R.

Gila Cliff Dwellings National Monment

Gila R.

Truth or Consequences

Elephant Butte Reservoir

Caballo Reservoir

Tularosa

Ruidoso

Alamogordo

Roswell

Roswell Museum and Art Center

International UFO Museum

Lovington

Artesia

Rio Penasco

Hobbs

Silver City

City of Rocks State Park

White Sands National Monument

Lake McMillan

Lordsburg

Rio Grande

Las Cruces

Deming

Carlsbad Caverns National Park

Carlsbad

Pecos R.

career doing experiments nearby. On display are many of his rockets and a replica of his workshop.

West of Roswell you pass through mile upon mile of dry, hilly rangeland before finally climbing into the greenery of the Capitan Mountains. There, you will find the tiny town of Lincoln, where Billy the Kid once wreaked havoc. All of Lincoln—it only has one street—is now a state monument, and you can tread the rough floors of the courthouse where the Kid made his violent escape.

Southwest of Lincoln is another of New Mexico's extraordinary natural wonders. White Sands National Monument is 230 square miles of brilliant white sand dunes made of a mineral called gypsum. Near the park's edge, where the dunes are flatter, a few plants and animals manage to eke out an existence. But in the center of the white expanse, where the strong, steady winds sometimes move the dunes ten feet per year, plants cannot grow fast enough to take root and survive. In some places in the park you can see nothing but the waves of white around you and hear nothing but the wind whistling across the sand. Building sand castles at the monument is out of the question, because there is no water to hold the sand together. But clambering up the steep dunes and running madly back down them again offers plenty of fun.

Farther west, in the majestic Gila National Forest, is Gila Cliff Dwellings National Monument. About seven hundred years ago, a band of Mogollon built houses in natural caves in a cliff high above a canyon floor. Exploring the caves provides a close-up look at the ancient walls the Mogollon built. Soot from their fires still stains the ceilings and remnants of tools and corncobs lie in corners.

As you come down from the mountains and head north, the land

The lonely landscape of White Sands National Monument

opens up. On the immense empty plains west of Socorro twenty-seven huge dish antennas comprise the world's largest radio telescope, called the Very Large Array (VLA). Each antenna measures eighty-two feet across and weighs more than two hundred tons. They pick up radio waves from distant galaxies, which can tell scientists much about the history of the universe. Inside the VLA visitor center, exhibits explain how radio telescopes

At Gila Cliff Dwellings National Monument, a steep stairway leads up to the houses built by the Mogollon seven hundred years ago.

The world's largest radio telescope is made up of twenty-seven giant dish antennas spread out across an empty plain in New Mexico.

work and how the antennas are put together. More awe-inspiring is walking to one of the giant antennas, trying to imagine what it is hearing from the far reaches of the universe.

CENTRAL NEW MEXICO

The massive bluff called El Morro National Monument provides vivid evidence of New Mexico's long history. A thousand years ago,

Anasazi scratched pictures in the rock. In 1605, Juan de Oñate carved a message into the soft sandstone in large, loopy letters. Over the centuries, many other explorers, traders, and settlers followed suit, letting the world know that they, too, had stopped at what is now known as Inscription Rock.

Farther east is Acoma Pueblo. Often called Sky City, Acoma sits atop a massive sandstone rock rising 357 feet above the surrounding plain. This site was once home to 1,500 people, but now only about thirteen families live atop the mesa, which has no running water or electricity. The other Acomas live in modern communities on the valley floor. Historians estimate that the Acomas have been living in Sky City since A.D. 1100, but some people say they have been there since 800. Acoma claims to be the oldest continuously occupied city in the present-day United States. "The people at Hopi Mesa in Arizona and Taos Pueblo will tell you they are the oldest," says the Acoma guide, smiling slyly and wagging his finger. "But don't you believe them. No. Acoma is the oldest." Walking through Acoma's dusty streets past adobe houses and round stone ovens called hornos, the village does seem like it has been there forever.

Even more impressive than Acoma's age is its location. Standing at the edge of the rock offers a startling view of the ground far below, other extraordinary rock formations rising from the plain, and white-capped mountains in the distance. It might also offer the chance to look a soaring hawk straight in the eye.

Until a road was built in the 1940s, the Acomas had to carry everything they needed—food, water, building materials, even dirt for their cemetery—up a steep narrow path of treacherous steps worn into the soft sandstone. Taking this ancient path back down

Acoma Pueblo sits on top of a huge rock in western New Mexico.

from Acoma, you'll find yourself instinctively reaching for the hand-holds dug by countless hands into the walls over the centuries.

Albuquerque, New Mexico's largest city by far, spreads out at the base of the Sandia Mountains. Although much of Albuquerque is modern, you can savor the past in Old Town, a pleasant area of narrow streets and small shops surrounding a peaceful plaza. Else-

Every weekend, dances are demonstrated at Albuquerque's Pueblo Indian Cultural Center.

where in Albuquerque, the Indian Pueblo Cultural Center features displays of jewelry, pottery, and other artifacts from each pueblo. This provides an excellent chance to compare the pottery styles of New Mexico's nineteen pueblos. Every weekend the cultural center hosts traditional dance performances.

For a stunning view, take the Sandia Peak Aerial Tramway, a cable car that quickly rises four thousand feet from Albuquerque's desert landscape to the chilly, pine forests at the top of Sandia Peak.

If you're not crazy about heights, you can drive up, too, but it takes much longer.

Each October, the Albuquerque International Balloon Fiesta attracts people from far and wide to watch five hundred colorful hot-air balloons float gracefully against the brilliant blue sky. This is the world's largest balloon festival and is often touted as the world's most photographed event.

The Sandia Peak Aerial Tramway offers a spectacular view of the countryside near Albuquerque.

Albuquerque is renowned for its annual balloon festival—the world's largest.

Most people find little to lure them off the freeway on the long drive from Albuquerque to the Texas border, but the small town of Tucumcari does have one wonderfully weird site that shouldn't be missed. The Tucumcari Historical Research Institute is unlike any other museum you've ever seen. Where else could you find displays of barbed wire, old saddles, bottles, and fishing hats? Housing an amazing jumble of junk—perhaps whatever happened to be in somebody's barn—the museum offers a glimpse of the New Mexico that doesn't appear in tourist brochures.

SANTA FE AND BEYOND

When most people think of New Mexico, they think of Santa Fe and its muted adobe buildings nestled in the hills. The heart of Santa Fe is the Plaza, a lovely, grassy square where natives and tourists alike can while away a pleasant afternoon. Santa Fe, the oldest capital city in the United States, is home to the Palace of Governors, the nation's oldest continuously used public building, which was erected in 1610. The palace is now the State History

TEN LARGEST CITIES

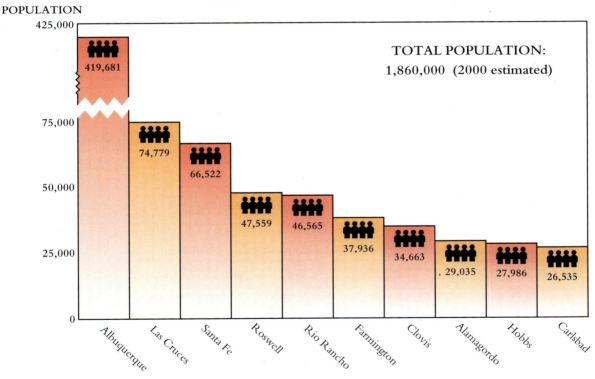

POPULATION

TOTAL POPULATION:
1,860,000 (2000 estimated)

City	Population
Albuquerque	419,681
Las Cruces	74,779
Santa Fe	66,522
Roswell	47,559
Rio Rancho	46,565
Farmington	37,936
Clovis	34,663
Alamagordo	29,035
Hobbs	27,986
Carlsbad	26,535

Museum for New Mexico and has exhibits detailing the region's history since the Spaniards arrived. Displays range from a reconstruction of a colonial chapel to unusual frontier objects such as a rawhide violin and a chandelier made from tin cans.

Another Santa Fe highlight is the Loretto Chapel and its famous "miraculous staircase." This elegant spiral staircase, which rises to the choir loft, was built without any nails or central support. The only thing holding it up is the quality of its craftsmanship. According to legend, the staircase was built by a traveling carpenter, who disappeared after finishing the job without so much as leaving his name, much less accepting payment.

North of Santa Fe, in Ranchos de Taos, stands one of the most extraordinary buildings in New Mexico. Built in 1730, the pure, abstract form of the church of San Francisco de Asis is more sculpture than architecture. Its plain brown adobe walls lack the sharp corners and flat surfaces of most buildings. Instead, they curve toward the bright blue sky. That they are four feet thick and uncluttered by any windows only adds to their power. "One almost shakes in its presence," architectural historian G. E. Kidder once wrote.

Taos Pueblo, another of New Mexico's magnificent architectural accomplishments, lies farther north. A sprawling collection of adobe buildings, the pueblo is an endlessly captivating array of angles and corners. The village has sat at the same spot since the 1300s. One Taos Indian says, "The story of my people and the story of this place are one single story. No man can think of us without thinking of this place. We are always joined together."

Not far from Taos, Bandelier National Monument in lovely

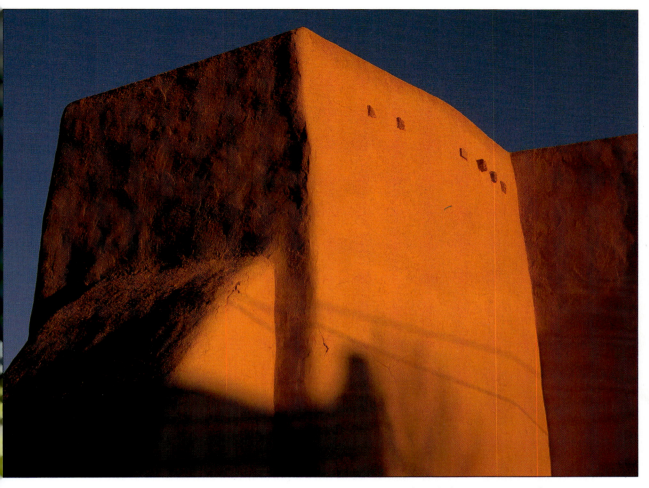

The abstract forms of the San Franscisco de Asis church have captivated many painters. "Most artists who spend any time in Taos have to paint it, I suppose, just as they have to paint a self-portrait," Georgia O'Keeffe once said. "I had to paint it—the back of it several times, the front once."

Frijoles Canyon boasts an impressive group of Anasazi ruins and cave dwellings. The canyon's cliffs are made of volcanic ash. Over the course of hundreds of thousands of years, the ash was pressed together into a soft pink and white rock called tuff, which wears

At Bandelier, the Anasazi built multistory dwellings against the soaring cliffs. The smaller holes in the cliffs supported rows of floor and ceiling beams.

away easily. So many holes have developed in the walls of Frijoles Canyon that they look like Swiss cheese. The Anasazi took full advantage of this, hollowing out some of the holes further and building dwellings inside them. On the canyon floor are the ruins of a four-hundred-room village. You can still see the town's central plaza, the round kivas dug into the ground, and remnants of the ancient walls.

The most amazing spot at Bandelier is the ceremonial cave, which lies 150 feet above the canyon floor and can only be reached by climbing a series of rough ladders up the cliff wall. Unless you have a horrible fear of heights, it is well worth the effort. The ceremonial cave is the perfect place to sit, relax, and listen to the wind rustling through the leaves, the birds twittering, and the rain softly falling, and imagine what life was like for the people who lived in this stunning spot centuries ago.

Bandelier is on the eastern edge of the Jemez Mountains, which abound with outdoor activities: fishing for trout in clear streams, hiking through dense pine forests past outcroppings of brilliant red rocks, or simply relaxing in the cool shade of dark green trees. These mountains also offer more exotic surprises. The unusual natural formation called the Soda Dam was created over thousands of years by the buildup of minerals from nearby springs. The weird mushroom-shaped formation now blocks most of the Jemez River, forcing the water to gush through the one tunnel it has eroded in the dam. Although the Soda Dam is fascinating to look at and fun to walk on, you might not want to hang around too long—it smells terrible. The minerals in the dam give it a sulfury aroma.

A better place to loiter is Spence Hot Springs. A million years ago, volcanic explosions created the Jemez Mountains. Today, deep underground, hot pockets still boil and bubble, creating the region's many hot springs. Spence Hot Springs is a beautiful series of pools set among boulders, where the hot water falls from one to another, like a fabulous 104-degree shower. No signs point to Spence Hot Springs, so only people who have been told by someone else know where to pull off the road. Those who find it can lounge in the warm bubbling water and watch the light of day fade, with only the peaceful forest and lovely mountains in view—not a car, a road, or a building in sight.

In New Mexico's northwest corner, down twenty miles of unpaved road that turns to impassable mud with the coming of rain, lies Chaco Canyon, the site of the Anasazi's greatest achievement. Chaco Canyon was a political, religious, and trade center for the Anasazi. Perfectly straight roads, some thirty feet wide, extended to communities as far as forty-two miles away. No one knows why the Anasazi put so much effort into building the roads, since they had no carts or other vehicles that required them. Between A.D. 900 and 1200, the Anasazi built great apartment buildings at Chaco. The largest of these, Pueblo Bonito, contained more than six hundred rooms. As many as five thousand people lived at Chaco, making it the largest settlement in the future United States prior to the arrival of Europeans.

Although the Anasazi are long gone, the ruins of their incredible buildings remain. Wandering through Chaco Canyon, the first thing that strikes you is the sheer size of the structures. But on closer inspection you may notice that Anasazi masonry is extraordinary. Beauty seemed almost as important to them as function, for they put the rocks together in careful patterns.

Ruins of the Anasazi's vast structures still stand at Chaco Canyon.

Chaco Canyon is scrubby, high desert punctuated by rocky mesas. Looking out over the barren landscape, it is hard to understand why the Anasazi didn't choose somewhere more welcoming—somewhere with water, with trees—for their most elaborate city. Why did the Anasazi choose this site and why did they abandon it? Mysteries such as these reawaken your sense of New Mexico as a Land of Enchantment.

THE FLAG: *The flag shows a red Zia Indian sun symbol – a circle with four radiating points – on a field of yellow. It was adopted in 1925.*

THE SEAL: *In the center of the seal are two eagles. The larger American bald eagle, arrows clutched in its talons, protects the smaller Mexican eagle. Underneath is a scroll with the state motto. The seal was adopted in 1912.*

STATE SURVEY

Statehood: January 6, 1912

Origin of Name: Spanish explorers considered the region an additional part of Mexico.

Nickname: Land of Enchantment

Capital: Santa Fe

Motto: It Grows as It Goes

Colors: Red and yellow

Bird: Roadrunner

Animal: Black bear

Fish: New Mexico cutthroat trout

Insect: Tarantula hawk wasp

Flower: Yucca

Yucca

O, FAIR NEW MEXICO

In 1915, Elizabeth Garrett, the blind daughter of famed Sheriff Pat Garrett, wrote this song, which was adopted as the official state song in 1917. New Mexico also has a state song in Spanish, "Así Es Nuevo Méjico," adopted

Words & Music by
Elizabeth Garrett

Un - der a sky of az-ure, Where balm-y breez - es

blow; Kissed by the gold - en sun - shine,

Is Nu - e - vo Me-ji-co. Home of the Mon - te -

zu - ma, With fier-y heart a - glow.

State of the deeds his - tor-ic, Is Nue-vo Me - ji -

in 1971; a state ballad, "Land of Enchantment," adopted in 1989; and a state poem, "A Nuevo Mexico" ("To New Mexico"), written in 1911 and adopted in 1991.

Turquoise

Tree: Piñon

Vegetables: Chiles and pinto beans

Grass: Blue grama

Gem: Turquoise

Fossil: Coelophysis dinosaur

Cookie: Bizcochito

Poem: "A Nuevo Mexico" by Luis Tafoya

GEOGRAPHY

Highest Point: 13,161 feet, at Wheeler Peak in Taos County

Lowest Point: 2,817 feet, at Red Bluff Reservoir in Eddy County

Area: 121,598 square miles

Greatest Distance, North to South: 395 miles

Greatest Distance, East to West: 355 miles

Bordering States: Colorado to the north, Oklahoma to the east, Texas to the east and south, and Arizona to the west

Hottest Recorded Temperature: 116°F at Artesia on June 29, 1918, and at Orogrande on July 14, 1934

Coldest Recorded Temperature: -50°F at Gavilan on February 1, 1951

Average Annual Precipitation: 13 inches

Major Rivers: Canadian, Gila, Pecos, Rio Grande, San Juan

Major Lakes: Bottomless Lakes, Conchas Reservoir, Elephant Butte Reservoir, Lake Sumner, Navajo Reservoir

Trees: blue spruce, desert willow, Douglas fir, juniper, piñon, ponderosa pine, Rio Grande cottonwood

Wild Plants: creosote bush, desert marigold, desert zinnia, fishhook barrel cactus, mesquite, sunset cactus, yucca

Animals: antelope, Barbary sheep, bighorn sheep, bobcat, brown bear, coyote, elk, fox, jackrabbit, lizard, mink, mountain lion, mule deer, muskrat, prairie dog, rattlesnake

Birds: crane, duck, hawk, heron, hummingbird, owl, pelican, roadrunner, sandpiper, tern, wild turkey, woodpecker

Coyote

Fish: bass, bream, catfish, crappie, perch, pike, trout

Endangered Animals: American peregrine falcon, bald eagle, Gila trout, least tern, Mexican long-nosed bat, Mexican spotted owl, New Mexican ridge-nosed rattlesnake, Southwestern willow flycatcher, whooping crane

New Mexican ridge-nosed rattlesnake

Endangered Plants: gypsum wild-buckwheat, Knowlton cactus, Kuenzler hedgehog cactus, Lee pincushion cactus, Lloyd's hedgehog cactus, Lloyd's mariposa cactus, Mesa Verde cactus, Sacramento Mountains thistle, Sacramento prickly-poppy, Sneed pincushion cactus

TIMELINE

New Mexico History

A.D. **900–1300** The Anasazi build a network of hundreds of stone buildings in Chaco Canyon

1200–1500 Pueblo Indians establish villages along the Rio Grande

1536 Alvar Núñez Cabeza de Vaca, Esteban the Moor, and two others possibly cross what is now southern New Mexico before arriving in Mexico

1540–1542 Francisco Vásquez de Coronado explores the area from the Gulf of California to present-day Kansas, including New Mexico

1598 Juan de Oñate establishes San Juan de los Caballeros, the first Spanish colony in New Mexico

1609–1610 Gaspar de Villagra publishes an epic history of the founding of New Mexico, the first book printed about any area in the United States

1680 Pueblo Indian revolt expels all Spaniards from New Mexico

1692 Don Diego de Vargas reconquers New Mexico for Spain

1706 Albuquerque is founded

1776 Franciscan friars Dominquez and Escanté explore route from New Mexico to California

1807 Zebulon Pike leads first Anglo-American expedition into New Mexico

1821 Mexico declares independence from Spain; Santa Fe Trail opens

1846 Mexican-American War begins; Stephen Watts Kearny annexes New Mexico into the United States

1848 Treaty of Guadalupe Hidalgo ends Mexican-American War

1850 New Mexico, which included present-day Arizona, southern Colorado, southern Utah, and southern Nevada, is designated a U.S. territory

1851 Bishop Jean Baptiste Lamy arrives in New Mexico and establishes schools, hospitals, and orphanages throughout the territory

1853 The Gadsden Purchase from Mexico adds 45,000 square miles to the territory

1861 After the outbreak of the Civil War, Confederates invade New Mexico from Texas and declare the Confederate Territory of Arizona

1862 Union troops twice defeat Confederates ending Confederate occupation of New Mexico

1862–1866 Navajos and Apaches are relocated by U.S. government to Bosque Redondo Reservation; thousands die of disease and starvation

1879 The Atlantic & Pacific Railroad (later renamed the Santa Fe Railroad) arrives in New Mexico, opening full-scale trade and migration of settlers from the East and Midwest

1881 Billy the Kid is killed by Sheriff Pat Garrett

1886 Apache leader Geronimo surrenders, ending Indian hostilities in the Southwest

1912 New Mexico becomes the 47th state

1916 Mexican revolutionary Pancho Villa raids Columbus, New Mexico

1917 Socialite Mabel Dodge Luhan invites artists such as Ansel Adams and Georgia O'Keeffe to Taos, which becomes known as an artists' haven

1923 Oil is discovered on the Navajo Reservation

1942 Los Alamos is selected as the secret site for the development of the atomic bomb

1945 World's first atomic bomb is detonated in southern New Mexico

1948 Native Americans win the right to vote in state elections

1966 New state capitol building is dedicated

1982 Space shuttle *Columbia* lands at White Sands Space Harbor

1998 New Mexico celebrates 400th anniversary of the founding of the first Spanish colony in the region

ECONOMY

Agricultural Products: cattle, chiles, corn, cotton, hay, milk, onions, pecans, poultry, sheep, wheat, wool

Cattle ranch

Manufactured Products: communication equipment, construction materials, electronic components, food processing, petroleum refining, precision instruments

Natural Resources: copper, gold, iron ore, lead, manganese, molybdenum, natural gas, oil, potash, sand and gravel, silver, uranium, zinc

Business and Trade: banking, processed natural resources, real estate, research, tourism

CALENDAR OF CELEBRATIONS

New Year's Day Celebration A mass, procession, and traditional dances such as the Turtle and Matachines dances celebrate the beginning of a new year at Picurís Pueblo south of Taos.

Mardi Gras in the Mountains This celebration is held in the Red River Ski Basin from late February until early March. It features parades on the ski slopes, balls in the lodges, winter cookouts, snow-sculpture competitions, and sled rides for families.

Chama Winter Carnival The winter carnival in Chama in late February and early March includes snowmobile races, dances, and cross-country ski competitions.

Dinosaur Days In mid-April, an open-air bazaar in Clayton includes an Old Western Dance, complete with costumes and prizes. Visitors can also take free tours of prehistoric dinosaur tracks in Clayton Lake State Park.

Taos Spring Arts Festival This May festival in Taos includes an arts-and-crafts show and many gallery openings and museums exhibitions.

Las Vegas Rails 'n' Trails Days Each June, a fiddlers' contest, barbecue, rodeo, and country-and-western dancing commemorate the historic Santa Fe Trail and the arrival of the railroad in Las Vegas.

Clovis Music Festival Rock 'n' roll greats such as Buddy Holly and Roy Orbison recorded their hits at Norman Petty's recording studio in Clovis. This festival, held in mid-July, celebrates the music of the 1950s with outdoor dances, an antique auto show, and live music performances.

San Juan County Fair Farmington is the site of the largest county fair in New Mexico each August. This weeklong event features concerts, livestock shows, exhibits, a fiddling contest, a parade, an arts-and-crafts show, and a carnival.

Intertribal Indian Ceremonial In late August New Mexico's oldest all-Indian exhibition attracts tribe members and visitors from across the United States, Canada, and Mexico to a powwow, rodeo, Indian arts-and-crafts show, and parade in Gallup.

Mountain Man Rendezvous and Buffalo Roast The rough-and-tumble life of mountain men is the theme of this Santa Fe event in late August. It features traditional music, blacksmithing, tomahawk throwing, and a mountain man's dinner featuring wild game dishes such as rattlesnake, elk, rabbit, grouse, deer, and buffalo.

Santa Fe Indian Market First held in 1922, this late August exhibition of Native American art is the oldest and largest in the world. Displays include handmade baskets, pottery, rugs, jewelry, drums, kachina dolls, sandpainting, and much more.

Fiesta de Santa Fe The oldest community festival in the nation commemorates the reconquest of New Mexico by Don Diego de Vargas in 1692. The pageantry includes the arrival of the Fiesta Queen and her court, reenactments of Don Diego's arrival in Santa Fe, and the burning of Zozobra (Old Man Gloom). The fiesta is held the weekend after Labor Day.

Staked Plains Roundup Horse lovers will enjoy the cowboy poetry, western music, saddle making, boot making, blacksmithing, rawhide braiding, and horse shows at this event held near Hobbs in late September.

Albuquerque International Balloon Fiesta Each October, Albuquerque hosts the world's biggest balloon fiesta, which features hundreds of hot-air balloons. Although not a race, prizes are awarded to balloonists who can land closest to target areas or snatch objects off the ground while in low flight.

Albuquerque International Balloon Fiesta

Cloudcroft Oktoberfest Hayrides, food booths, square dances, nature tours, a horseshoe tournament, and an art competition are some of the attractions at this October event in Cloudcroft.

Festival of the Cranes This November event celebrates the return of tens of thousands of sandhill cranes, along with other species including snow geese, bald eagles, wild turkeys, and whooping cranes to the Bosque del Apache National Wildlife Refuge in San Antonio for the winter. There are workshops, tours, and children's events such as nature walks, films, and puppet shows.

Indian National Finals Rodeo The best Native American rodeo riders from the United States and Canada compete for the title of World Champion Indian Cowboy in mid-November in Albuquerque.

Shalako Ceremony and Dance In early December, six ten-foot-tall masked dancers wearing colorful costumes begin a nightlong house-blessing ceremony by crossing a small river that runs through Zuñi Pueblo. Visitors from around the world come to see this solemn event.

Christmas at the Palace The Governor's Palace in Santa Fe is the site of traditional holiday festivities in mid-December, including storytelling, candle lighting, music, and the serving of bizcochitos, coffee, and cider.

STATE STARS

Rudolfo Anaya (1937–   ) was born in Pastura and became a teacher and school counselor before turning to writing. His novels *Bless Me, Ultima* and *Tortuga*, which draw heavily on his Latino heritage, have won many awards.

William H. Bonney (1859?–1881), who was better known as Billy the Kid, was born in New York and came to New Mexico as a child. As a teenager, he became a gambler, a killer, and a ringleader in the cattle wars between ranchers. When Bonney escaped from prison after being convicted of murder, Sheriff Pat Garrett tracked him down and shot him dead in Fort Sumner.

Fernando E. Cabeza de Baca (1937–   ), born in Albuquerque, is a direct descendant of the Spanish explorer of the same name. He served in the army during the Vietnam War and then was appointed a special assistant by President Gerald Ford in 1974, making him the youngest and highest-ranking federal executive of Hispanic descent.

Kit Carson (1809–1868) ran away from his home in Missouri at age 16 and became a trapper and trader along the Santa Fe Trail. He was also an Indian fighter who forced the Navajo across New Mexico in the Long Walk. He was a frontier hero and a legend in his day.

Willa Cather (1873–1947) was living in New Mexico looking for subjects for her stories when she learned how Bishop Lamy had built schools and orphanages in New Mexico. His life gave her the idea for a novel that became an American classic, *Death Comes for the Archbishop*. Cather was born in Winchester, Virginia.

Willa Cather

John Simpson Chisum (1824–1884) was the first cattle rancher in New Mexico. Moving his cattle operation from Texas, Chisum settled permanently at South Spring near Roswell. When the cattle wars broke out, he led the movement to restore law and order, hiring Sheriff Pat Garrett to hunt down Billy the Kid. Chisum afterwards became known as the Cattle King.

John Denver (1943–1997) started out as a folksinger
with the Chad Mitchell Trio. After going solo in 1968,
he composed and recorded a number of hits including "Leaving on a Jet Plane," "Rocky Mountain High,"
and "Annie's Song." He was active in many causes,
including UNICEF, Friends of the Earth, and Save the
Children. Denver was born in Roswell.

John Denver

Greer Garson (1908–1996) emigrated from
Ireland and made her reputation in Hollywood as a leading lady in such films as *Mrs.
Miniver*, *Random Harvest*, and *Madame Curie*.
She was nominated for the Oscar every year
between 1941 and 1945. She eventually
retired to New Mexico, where she and her
husband became involved in environmental
causes, donating hundreds of acres of their
property to the state park system.

Greer Garson

R. C. Gorman (1932–   ) is an internationally known Navajo artist.
His most popular works are lithographs, woodblocks, and charcoal por-
trayals of people often caught in reflective moments and natural settings.
In 1973, he became the first living Native American artist to have his
work on permanent display in the Metropolitan Museum of Art in New
York City.

Tony Hillerman (1925–) is the author of more than 15 best-selling mystery novels, which concentrate on the clash between modern society and traditional Navajo values and customs. His novels, such as *Skinwalkers* and *Talking God*, display a deep understanding of Navajo culture. Hillerman lives in Albuquerque.

Conrad Hilton (1887–1979), who was born in San Antonio, New Mexico, helped run his father's businesses, which included renting rooms to migrant workers. After serving in World War I, Hilton invested in a small hotel. By the 1960s, his Hilton Hotel chain was one of the largest chains of luxury hotels in the world. He told his story in a popular book about putting customers first, *Be My Guest*.

Dolores Huerta (1930–), a labor organizer, was born in Dawson, a small mining town in northern New Mexico. Her mother ran a boardinghouse for migrant workers. Later, Huerta joined Cesar Chavez in building the National Farm Workers Association (now called the United Farm Workers of America), which waged a difficult but ultimately successful campaign to improve the working conditions of migrant workers in the Southwest.

Dolores Huerta (third from right)

Jean Baptiste Lamy (1814–1888), a Catholic bishop born in France, was sent by the Vatican to Santa Fe in 1851. He arrived to find 14 priests serving a region sprawled over five states. He built schools, hospitals, and churches. His work was the basis of Willa Cather's novel *Death Comes for the Archbishop*.

Nancy Lopez (1957–   ), one of the best golfers ever, moved to Roswell from Torrence, California, as a young girl. Her parents, avid golfers, taught her to play. She developed into a record-breaking professional golfer, winning 2 national amateur championships and 48 professional golf tournaments. Lopez was inducted into the Ladies Professional Golf Hall of Fame in 1987 when she was 30 years old.

Manuelito (1818–1893) was a Navajo leader who led an attack on Fort Defiance in Arizona. Later he successfully persuaded federal authorities to allow the Navajo to return to their homeland after the Long Walk to Bosque Redondo Reservation.

Maria Martinez (1887–1980) was a leading Native American artist. Born in San Ildefonso Pueblo near Santa Fe, she made her first pottery as a child of seven or eight. Her elegant black-on-black pottery earned her worldwide renown.

Bill Mauldin (1921–   ) is a cartoonist who was born in Mountain Park. While serving in World War II, he drew cartoons about the true lives of battle-tired soldiers, which later appeared in St. Louis and Chicago newspapers. He won the Pulitzer Prize in 1945 and 1959.

N. Scott Momaday (1934–   ) writes poetry and fiction that reflect his Kiowa Indian heritage. He was born in Oklahoma, moved to Jemez Pueblo when he was 12, and later attended the University of New

Mexico. His Pulitzer Prize–winning novel, *House Made of Dawn*, is about the overlap of Indian and Anglo cultures.

Demi Moore (1962–   ), the star of such movies as *Ghost*, *A Few Good Men*, and *G.I. Jane*, was born in Roswell. After starting out in television on *General Hospital*, Moore became a major Hollywood actress in a few short years.

John Nichols (1940–   ) was born in Berkeley, California. At age 16, he got off a Greyhound bus in Taos and decided to stay. His New Mexican trilogy of novels, *The Milagro Beanfield War*, *The Magic Journey*, and *The Nirvana Blues*, are about the destruction of old cultures in the name of progress.

Georgia O'Keeffe (1887–1986), an artist, visited New Mexico in 1929, was enraptured, and spent much of the rest of her life there. She often looked to the desert for inspiration for her paintings, which usually featured bold, simplified images of objects from nature. Her works are displayed in museums all over the world.

Bobby Unser (1934–   ) and **Al Unser** (1939–   ), both born in Albuquerque, are the best- known members of a famous auto-racing family. Al Unser won the Indianapolis 500 four times; Bobby won it three times.

Pablita Velarde (1918–   ), an artist, was born at Santa Clara Pueblo. She uses raw colors from the earth in her paintings, grinding them into powders. She has been called the mother of Pueblo painting, because she introduced it to the world.

Lew Wallace (1827–1905) was a lawyer and a major general in the Civil War before becoming governor of the New Mexico Territory. During his

time as governor, he put an end to the cattle wars and wrote *Ben Hur*, a popular novel about Christians in ancient Rome.

Lew Wallace

TOUR THE STATE

Albuquerque Museum of Art, History, and Science (Albuquerque) This museum houses artifacts from 20,000 B.C. to the present, including Spanish colonial items, Native American arts, costumes, photographs, and crafts. The museum also has a special children's section, a library, and a sculpture garden.

Aztec Museum and Pioneer Village (Aztec) Step back in time by visiting a sheriff's office, jail, law office, doctor's office, blacksmith shop, and log cabin, all from around 1880. Museum displays include clocks, dolls, quilts, farm equipment, and other items used by pioneers.

Blue Hole (Santa Rosa) Fed by an underground river, this 81-foot-deep pool near Santa Rosa has crystal clear waters that remain a cool 61°F throughout the year. It attracts diving enthusiasts from all over the world.

Bosque del Apache (Socorro) This 57,000-acre national wildlife refuge along the Rio Grande is home to nearly 300 species of birds. The birds either live at the refuge or, like the endangered whooping crane, migrate through on a seasonal basis.

Bradbury Science Museum (Los Alamos) This museum details the secret development of the first atomic bomb. It also features exhibits about defense weapons, energy, and current scientific research.

Carlsbad Caverns National Park (Carlsbad) Twenty miles south of Carlsbad are the world's largest limestone caverns. The park preserves a network of 80 caves, some hundreds of feet high. A colony of hundreds of thousands of Mexican free-tail bats lives in the caverns.

The Catwalk (Glenwood) Twenty-five feet above tumbling Whitewater Creek in Gila National Forest, a metal walkway clings to the canyon walls. The sheer 250-foot bluffs seem to touch high above. Visitors enjoy hiking and picnicking along this colorful canyon.

Chaco Culture National Historical Park (Bloomfield) Chaco canyon preserves the ruins of hundreds of stone buildings, some four stories high, in what was the largest Anasazi settlement.

El Morro National Monument (Grants) Carved on this 200-foot-high sandstone wall are pictures made by prehistoric Indians, brave words by Spanish explorers, and autographs of westbound pioneers. You can walk around the rock and see the centuries roll past.

Fort Sumner (Fort Sumner) This former frontier military post served as a holding camp for thousands of Navajos during the 1860s, after they were forced to leave their homeland on the Long Walk. It is also the site of Billy the Kid's grave.

Gila Cliff Dwellings National Monument (Silver City) About 700 years ago, members of the Mogollon culture built homes in natural caves in a canyon wall 200 feet above the Gila River. Archaeologists have unearthed bowls, tools, and artwork in the 42 rooms of adobe brick.

International Space Hall of Fame (Alamogordo) This four-story golden cube contains exhibits about space exploration from the earliest days of rocketry to the present. Highlights include hands-on exhibits about piloting spacecrafts and the effects of weightlessness, a simulated walk on Mars, and a collection of video interviews with scientists and astronauts.

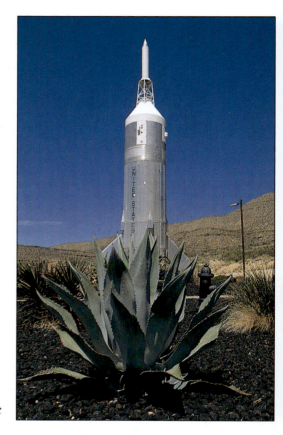

International Space Hall of Fame

International UFO Museum and Research Center (Roswell) Visitors to this museum can learn about alleged UFO sightings and the rumor that an alien spacecraft crashed nearby in 1947. Exhibits show documents claiming that the United States military covered up the crash and secretly examined bodies of aliens recovered at the site.

Las Cruces Museum of Natural History (Las Cruces) Dinosaur bones, fossilized trees, animal skeletons, and gems are all part of this museum dedicated to New Mexico's prehistoric past. The museum also hosts field trips to dig sites.

Rio Grande Zoological Park (Albuquerque) At this zoo, visitors can see more than 1,000 animals in displays that simulate their natural habitats, including an African savanna and a rain forest. The park also houses a children's zoo and offers educational programs.

Shiprock (Shiprock) A vertical shaft of rock that rises 1,500 feet above the desert floor, Shiprock is called *Tse Be dahi* (Winged Rock) in the Navajo language. Legend says this sacred landmark, 12 miles southwest of the town of Shiprock, once sprouted wings to carry the Navajo people to safety following an enemy attack.

Smokey Bear Historical State Park (Capitan) Smokey Bear was a real cub rescued from a forest fire near Capitan. The visitor center has exhibits about forest fires and fire prevention. Nearby is the grave of Smokey Bear.

Very Large Array (Socorro) is the world's most powerful radio telescope. The array is used by scientists from all over the world to examine deep space. The site was used in the films *Independence Day* and *Contact*. Self-guided tours are available.

War Eagles Museum (Santa Teresa) This museum displays fighter planes from World War II, jet fighters from the Korean War, and antique automobiles.

FUN FACTS

More painters, sculptors, poets, musicians, dancers, and filmmakers live in north-central New Mexico than in any other area of roughly the same size in the United States.

Constructed in 1610, the Governor's Palace in Santa Fe is the oldest continuously occupied public building in the United States. It has been the home of Spanish and Mexican governors, as well as headquarters for Pueblo Indians, the U.S. Army, and the Confederate army. Currently, the palace houses a museum.

El Camino Real (the Royal Road), which ran from Mexico City to Santa Fe, was the first road established by Europeans in the present-day United States. Travelers began using it in about 1581.

FIND OUT MORE

If you want to learn more about New Mexico, check your local library, bookstore, or video store for these titles:

GENERAL INTEREST BOOKS

Ayer, Eleanor H. *The Anasazi*. New York: Walker and Company, 1993.

Berry, Michael. *Georgia O'Keeffe*. New York: Chelsea House, 1988.

Lavender, David. *The Santa Fe Trail*. New York: Holiday House, 1995.

Marrin, Albert. *Empires Lost and Won: The Spanish Heritage in the Southwest*. New York: Atheneum, 1997.

Melody, Michael E. *The Apache*. New York: Chelsea House, 1989.

Streissguth, Tom. *Rocket Man: The Story of Robert Goddard*. Minneapolis: Carolrhoda Books, 1995.

FICTION

Anaya, Rudolfo. *Bless Me, Ultima*. New York: Warner Books, 1972, 1994. A classic coming-of-age novel.

Bogard, Larry. *Los Alamos Light*. New York: Farrar, Straus, & Giroux, 1983.

A young girl is forced to move to New Mexico when her father begins doing secret research at Los Alamos during World War II.

Mazzio, Joann. *Leaving Eldorado*. Boston: Houghton Mifflin, 1993. A fourteen-year-old girl struggles with life in an 1880s New Mexican mining town.

———. *The One Who Came Back*. Boston: Houghton Mifflin, 1992. A mystery about a missing boy set in the mountains of New Mexico.

VIDEOS

Georgia O'Keeffe. Boston: Home Vision, 1977.

New Mexico. San Ramon, CA: International Video Network/Triad Productions, 1995.

A Tour of Santa Fe and the State of New Mexico. Memphis: City Productions Home Video, 1996.

INTERNET SITES

http://www.state.nm.us

This is the official website of the New Mexico state government.

http://www.newmexico.org

The New Mexico Department of Tourism site offers plenty of information on what to see and do in the state.

INDEX

Chart, graph, and illustration page numbers are in boldface.